CHOSEN BY GOD
CALLED BY GRACE
An Autobiography

PETER SCHULER

CHOSEN BY GOD, CALLED BY GRACE: AN AUTOBIOGRAPHY
by Peter Schuler

ISBNs: 978-1-953625-19-9 Trade Paperback | 978-1-953625-20-5 Ebook

Photographs by Peter Schuler.

Intelligent Design Press
An imprint of Kelley Creative
Spokane, Washington, USA

Chosen By God, Called by Grace

An Autobiography

by Peter Schuler

INTELLIGENT DESIGN PRESS

With God, all things are possible!

To all Believers who are chosen by God
to spend eternity in His glorious presence.

O God, Thou art my God, I seek Thee, my soul thirsts for
Thee; my flesh faints for Thee, as in a dry and weary land
where no water is. Psalm 63.1

Contents

Introduction

This autobiography is truly God's story written for me to fulfill His plan and purpose through my life, for the glory of His name. As I look back on my life, I realize that God has been working in everything for good to prepare me to fulfill His vision to send me to preach the Gospel to the world. Throughout the history of the Bible, God's plan has been accomplished through men and women who were chosen by Him. My journey of walking with God has been amazing, and the most incredible chapter has just begun! While writing this book, the Lord began to fulfill His vision from forty-four years ago, that He would send me to preach the Word to many nations. My heart was filled with joy when the Lord opened doors to do ten online crusades in Pakistan where hundreds of people have come to Christ and many have been healed and delivered from demons. Praise God!

I am truly blessed to have known my eternal heavenly Father. I love the Lord with all of my heart, mind, soul, and strength. In the midst of stage four cancer, I lift my hands and praise my eternal Father, the Creator of all things. I have incredible joy in my heart and nothing can separate me from His love. I will praise and serve Him until my last breath, when the Lord will receive me into His glorious presence. The Father will fulfill His promises and save me for His eternal purpose! Hallelujah!

The glory of God in last month's crusade in Pakistan

The Lord has called me to write three books that describe the Father's amazing plan written for my life. In the first book of this trilogy, ***In Pursuit of God: A Love Story***, I share my life-long journey to seek God with all of my heart. I reveal my love for Him and His love for me. I describe the joy of walking with God in the mountains, His amazing visions and revelations to me, my twenty-five years of ministry serving Jesus, and His healing of my terminal illness. Truly, God is good! My second book, ***Warrior for Christ: Overcoming Cancer by Faith***, is an inspirational story of walking by faith to overcome childhood oppression, a terminal illness, persecution, and spiritual warfare. The book also includes a detailed account of overcoming stage four cancer which caused eleven compression fractures of my vertebrae. I share advice on how to maintain a positive attitude, live by faith, rely on Christ for strength, and remain thankful while experiencing suffering. Finally, ***Chosen by God: Called by Grace***, is an account of God's call on my life to preach the Gospel to many nations and His plan to prepare me for this amazing ministry. I describe how the Lord has used every experience in my life to equip me to carry His Gospel to the world and gather His Church for the coming of Christ. The Father's plan has been to deliver me from childhood oppression, heal me from a terminal illness, call me to minister to the homeless for twenty-five years, and empower me to overcome stage four cancer by faith. I describe my friendship with the Father and the joy of walking with Him in His glorious creation. After forty-four years, the Lord has graciously called me to preach online to thousands of people at many crusades in Pakistan. In the midst of cancer and pain, the Lord has anointed me to lead hundreds to Christ, heal the sick, cast out demons, and baptize many in the Holy Spirit. Thank you Jesus for your grace and faithfulness! Lord, You are amazing!

Arise, shine; for your light has come, and the glory of the LORD has risen upon you. Isaiah 60.1

1

Called out of Darkness

"If the world hates you, know that it has hated me before it hated you. If you were of the world, the world would love its own; but because you are not of the world, but I chose you out of the world, therefore the world hates you"

John 15:18-19

"Do not think that I have come to bring peace on earth; I have not come to bring peace, but a sword. For I have come to set a man against his father, and a daughter against her mother, and a daughter-in-law against her mother-in-law; and a man's foes will be those of his own household.

Matthew 10:34-36

"Can a woman forget her sucking child, that she should have no compassion on the son of her womb: Even these may forget, yet I will not forget you. Behold, I have graven you on the palms of my hands; your walls are continually before me."

Isaiah 49:18-19

My journey to seek God began in my childhood of great darkness and oppression. I often felt lost in this cruel environment, but I now realize that God was working in all things for good. The Lord used this suffering to motivate me to seek God's with all of my heart. I was born into a family in Bellevue, Washington, which appeared normal on the outside, but there was evil hiding below the surface. My father had endured the Great Depression and as a teenager, he supported his family by selling newspapers and magazines. He was a radar specialist on a destroyer in the Battle of the Pacific, and he saved his ship several times by locating *kamikaze* planes that were seeking to destroy the vessel. My father came home eager to start the "American dream" family that was often portrayed on TV. America had won the war and there was a feeling of hope and prosperity. Unknown to him, his battle was just beginning. My dad opened an interior decorating business in Seattle and then started a real estate development business. He bought a small cabin on Lake Washington and completed several remodels and expansions. My father worked hard and experienced prosperity—on the surface we were living the "American dream." I experienced some enjoyable family camping trips and vacations to Europe, Hawaii, Canada, and Mexico. We periodically went fishing on Puget Sound for salmon, cod, and sole. I spent many days exploring Lake Washington with a small thirteen-foot Boston Whaler. I often took the small boat out during large storms so that I could jump the waves— one day I jumped too high and the engine fell off. In 1967, I attended a mock United Nations assembly for middle school students and I was selected as the delegate for Israel on the day that the Six-Day war commenced between Israel and the Arab coalition. It was an amazing experience. I became an eagle scout, and every year the scout troop spent a week hiking on a remote part of the Washington coast. We navigated by using tide charts because many on the beaches were only accessible during low tide. During this time, I obtained a Citizenship in the Nation merit badge from John Erlichman, who was involved in my scout troop in Bellevue, Washington. A couple of years later, he became the second most powerful man in the Nixon administration. After the Watergate scandal, I watched John on TV during the Senate investigations concerning the governmental corruption. That summer, our family traveled to Canada, and we stopped for lunch along the way at a café in Missoula, Montana. I was amazed to see John Erlichman eating at the same restaurant on his trip home from the Senate hearings. I mentioned that I had been watching him on TV and he seemed embarrassed. It was ironic to me that I was taught how to be a law-abiding citizen by a person who was later convicted of such political corruption. I enjoyed these trips to the mountains and the ocean, but there was an invisible enemy that was about to take control of this "happy family." This story is a warning to those who seek to build a kingdom on this earth without recognizing that we are in a spiritual war for our souls. My mother began to practice the power of positive thinking to achieve her goals. The Scriptures teach that where jealousy and selfish ambition exist, there will be disorder and every evil work (James 3:16). Evil was beginning to find a "doorway" into our family. My mother was not satisfied with these psychic abilities and she began to cross the line into demonic powers to achieve her objectives. She fell into the temptation of the enemy that you can be "like God, knowing good and evil." My mother was transformed into another person as the devil gained control over her life. She changed so dramatically that the children asked, "Who's that?" when we saw our mother on the home movies from several years earlier. Her demonic powers began to destroy the family. She no longer wanted to be married to her husband and I never saw them touch, kiss, sit together, or act affectionately towards each other. She refused to sleep with him for the last nineteen years of his life. She did, however, want his money, and she developed a plan to drive him out of the house and take everything. She did not permit him to talk about himself or his business in his own house. He no longer felt welcome at home, and her hate and abuse forced him to spend the last ten years of his life traveling for his business and living out of a small "carry-on" suitcase. She was able to turn his son and daughter against him and his "American dream" had become an "American nightmare." When he did try to visit, they were rude and disrespectful and often left him alone in the house. He would tell me, "it is better if I don't go home."

My father spent the remainder of his life depressed, traveling alone and surrounded by business associates who were thieves. He was not allowed to call me at the house and he was forced to drive to a payphone to talk to me. She tried to keep us apart because she was afraid that he would share some of the inheritance with me. My brother used deception to manipulate my father into giving him money and he would threaten to commit suicide if my dad didn't give him what he wanted. I lived in relative poverty while my father gave him a two-ton truck, a motorhome, and his own house. They preyed upon my father's kindness and generosity. My mother began to practice witchcraft against him and would often feel weak, sick, or extremely cold when he came home. She would frequently mock him and call him names such as the "great white hope." He was opposed to a divorce for Biblical reasons and because it would cause him to lose most of his money by "freezing" his business assets. My father would often tell me that there were two types of people, "givers and takers." He had a kind and generous heart, but he was surrounded by a family and business partners who tried to steal everything that he owned. His secretary even took advantage of his kindness and stole a large amount of money. My dad was a salesman who could be extremely persuasive. For example, on a plane trip, we were flying home to Seattle with a stop in Portland, but my father was able to convince the passengers, crew, and even the pilot that we were flying directly to Seattle. The pilot contacted the aviation authorities who confirmed that they were scheduled to stop in Portland. He was very friendly and often talked to strangers wherever he went. Sadly, I don't think that he had any true friends. My father was a believer, but he lacked the spiritual discernment and strength to combat the evil that had taken over his family. He had persevered through the Depression and World War II, but he was unable to win the battle against the evil in his own home. My father spent his life loving, giving, and taking care of his family, yet they treated him with contempt and cruelty. They did not appreciate him and turned his life into a "living hell". The evil had worn him out, and for the last several years before his death, he would often say, "you won't have your old gray-haired dad around much longer." The Lord had revealed to him that his time on earth was coming to an end. My father loved God's creation and he enjoyed riding trail bikes. In 1979, the Lord took him home when he crashed on his motorcycle in his favorite area in Cooper Basin which was near Sun Valley. I believe that when he died, an angel appeared to him and carried him up to heaven where he belonged. I was very sad after his death, but I rejoiced that he was free from the oppression of this life. The enemy sought to destroy him because he was chosen by God. This world was not worthy of him.

My family was divided: my father and I were believers but the remainder of the family were deceived by the evil one. I looked for love from my family, but instead, I received rejection and hate. Jesus proclaimed, "Do not think that I have come to bring peace on earth; I have not come to bring peace, but a sword. For I have come to set a man against his father, and a daughter against her mother, and a daughter-in-law against her mother-in-law; and a man's foes will be those of his own household. He who loves father or mother more than me is not worthy of me; and he who loves son or daughter more than me is not worthy of me" (Matthew 10:34-37). After my father's death, an angry fight ensued over his money, and one extended member of the family contacted me because she was very concerned that they were going to "kill each other" over the inheritance. My family obtained all of his money, but the real treasure was knowing him. Unfortunately, some Christians today seek what Jesus can give them instead of a true relationship with Christ. At the time of his death, I was riding my motorcycle in France and I saw a glorious light shine through the clouds at the exact time when he passed away. I learned about his death from his secretary and I was never told by my family where he was buried. I do know that he is in heaven and that is all that matters. The Lord told me shortly after his death that "He wanted my father for reasons that I could not now know." When my dad entered heaven, he realized that the evil and darkness had deceived him and turned him against me. He prayed and the Lord allowed him to send a message to my wife and me that "we were right, he was wrong and that he was sorry." I will always love my father and I look forward to seeing him in heaven where we will enjoy eternity exploring God's beautiful new earth. This next photo was taken on Lake Washington near my home where I spent many hours crying out to God to deliver me from the darkness. The Lord heard my prayer, and He would soon deliver me from the oppression.

I have been crucified with Christ, it is no longer I who live, but Christ who lives in me...
Galatians 2.20

After my father left home, I became the principal target of the evil and oppression. For many years, my mother practiced witchcraft to attempt to kill me in my bed at night. She would often paralyze me and stop me from breathing. The Holy Spirit was with me and kept me alive by helping me to breathe just before I passed out. At the time, I didn't understand why this was happening, but years later, the Lord revealed the truth to me that she was practicing witchcraft against me from her bedroom across the hallway. During the day, I would see my mother standing in the kitchen in a demonic trance draining the life out of me to give herself the energy to live. This demonic "rape" left me feeling weak and exhausted. Throughout my childhood, I believed that God gave powers to every mother to read their children's minds so that they could discipline them. She would often yell at me for what I was thinking—I realized years later that her ability came from demons and not from God. I have experienced so much verbal abuse in this life that I still have difficulty listening to people who are yelling—even on a TV show or movie. She was a dictator who would attempt to control and manipulate every move that I made. She forced me to attend the same classes and read the same books that she liked as a child. She hated men and tried to turn me into a girl, which was one of the reasons that I was hated and bullied at school. She was so aggressive and domineering that my father would say that "she would have made a good man." She had always wanted to be a lawyer, and she gave me the option of going to law school or face being disowned. I lived under the constant threat that I would be thrown out on the street for any act of "disobedience." I was forced to obey the "dictator" because I was still young and unprepared for independent living. In the end, I was thrown out anyway for becoming a Christian, getting married, and "flunking out" of my last year of law school. Years later, the Lord made her confess that her abuse was completely unjustified because I had been a very good and obedient boy. The devil is a liar and so are those who follow him.

I was not able to physically grow or develop in this toxic environment of hate, anger, and condemnation. I was never touched, loved, encouraged, or comforted—even as a baby. My mother continually criticized and judged my words and actions. For many years, I believed that I could never be good enough to please people. I became shy, withdrawn, and afraid of people. My goal in school was to be

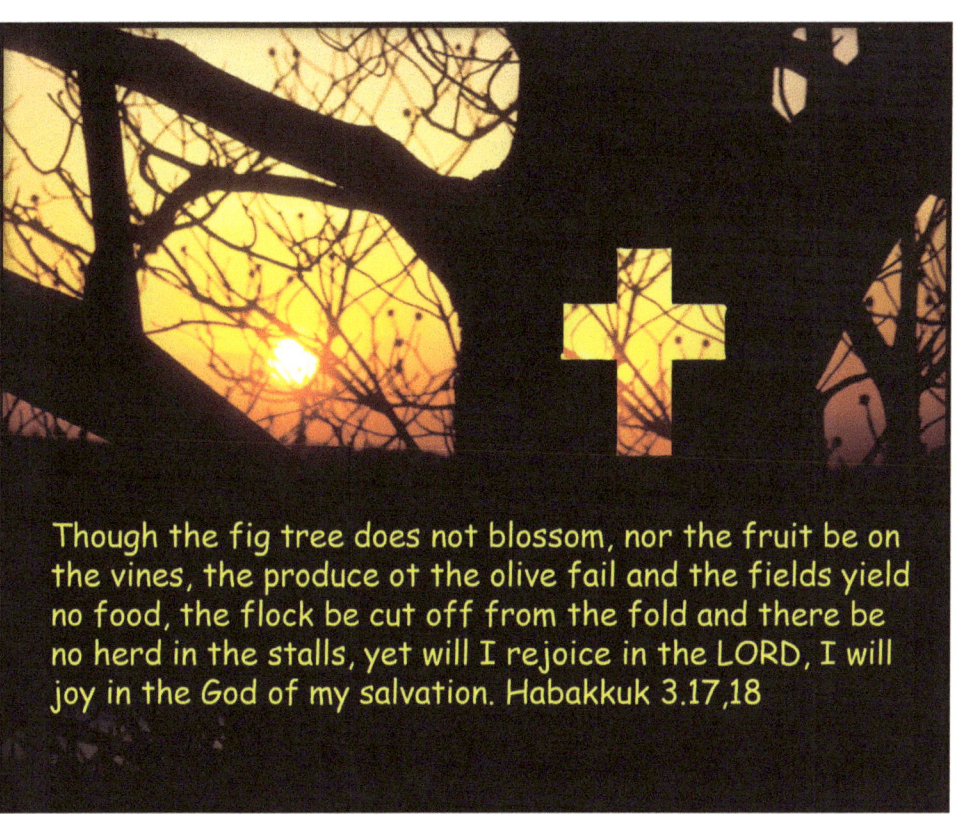

Though the fig tree does not blossom, nor the fruit be on the vines, the produce ot the olive fail and the fields yield no food, the flock be cut off from the fold and there be no herd in the stalls, yet will I rejoice in the LORD, I will joy in the God of my salvation. Habakkuk 3.17,18

This photo was taken on Lake Washington near my home.

invisible so that no one would mock, bully, or attack me. It seemed like my childhood was stolen from me. I was usually the last person picked for gym class and I did not do well in school. My mother told me that I was unable to do math because she had difficulty with this subject when she was young. In high school, I started a new math class with a teacher that I had never met. On the first day of class, he pointed me out as the "F" student because I looked like a failure to him. The high school counselor warned me not to go to college because I would "flunk out" of school. I spent many years believing that I was a "worthless failure." For this reason, I have always valued people who were encouragers. Several years ago, the Lord told me that most of the words that other people have spoken to me were words of Satan designed to tear down and destroy me.

My mother continued to attack me after I left home. When I was twenty-six years old, married and living in Idaho, she came to my door with an ax shaking in rage stating that "she had created me and that she was going to kill me." Apparently, in her mind, failure to attend a holiday meal deserved a death sentence. My dad saw her walk towards my door with an ax, but instead of stopping her, he just said, "one flew over a cuckoo's nest." My sister defended her right to attack me and replied, "that's not fair, dad." My father didn't try to stop the abuse and my sister supported it. The Lord would not let my mother harm me so she went home and used the ax to chop up a deck that I had built for them. Later, I asked God why I didn't grow up in a loving "Leave it to Beaver" (an idyllic Hollywood family on TV) home, and the Lord answered that I would have been comfortable and I would not have sought Him as I did. My mother continued to be angry with me throughout my life. For example, she went into a fit of anger demanding to have my camera and photographs because she had paid for them (when actually, my father had purchased them). My dad called and warned me that my mother was headed over to my place in an absolute rage (again, he didn't try to stop her). I told him that I would move to another town, but he replied that she was so angry that I should "move out of the county." God's grace protected me from harm through those years of anger and hostility. My family was extremely jealous of my trip to Europe and the pictures of my adventures in the mountains. The next year, they went to Europe with motorcycles and tried to retrace every step that I took on my trip. Their jealousy filled them with anger and hate and put them under the power of the evil one. My mother believed that their demonic powers would enable them to accomplish anything that I was able to achieve. In this family, I was always wrong and they were always right. My mother used my marriage as another excuse to disown me, but my brother was allowed to live with his girlfriend in her house. The day after my marriage, she sent me dead black roses with the inscription, "With God all things are possible." I was also disowned by her for not being able to complete my third year of law school, while my brother was accepted despite his failure to finish college. The rest of the family lived in luxury while I rented a single room near the university for fifty dollars a month and wore second-hand clothes from a thrift store. My classmates in my Church Bible school thought I was the poorest person in the class because of my modest lifestyle. I went back home for a weekend with one of my friends from school, who was surprised to see that my family was living a wealthy lifestyle. There was a definite "class system" in this family.

Most people don't grow up as a victim of witchcraft, but all of us start our lives in darkness because our sin separates us from God (Isaiah 59:1-3). The Word of God teaches that before our conversion, we were dead in sin, following the lusts of the flesh and the ways of this world. We were born into a world of darkness under the power of the enemy who blinded our eyes so that we could not see the light of the Gospel of the glory of Christ (2 Corinthians 4:4). God mercifully intervened to save us from eternal destruction. While we were yet sinners, Christ died for us and we are saved by His grace through faith and not by works (Ephesians 2:1-9). The Lord has created each of us with a need for a relationship with our Creator. All of us have a "God-shaped hole" within us that can only be filled with a personal relationship with Christ. Those who are separated from God have tried to fill this emptiness by "constructing" many gods out of their own imagination. There are thousands of counterfeit gods in this world, but there is only one true God who created all things (1 Corinthians 8:5-6). Many people try to fill this "God-shaped hole" with money, possessions, sex, drugs, and alcohol, but only Jesus can satisfy the emptiness. During my childhood, I spent countless hours at a nearby lake crying out to God to deliver me from the oppression. Because of the childhood trauma, I imagined that God was angry at me and that He wanted to "squash me like a bug" if I stepped on the wrong square on the floor. The Lord would soon answer my prayer and reveal His love and mercy to me.

2

Into the Light

"You will seek me and find me, when you seek me with all
your heart."

Jeremiah 29:13

"He has delivered us from the dominion of darkness and
transferred us to the kingdom of his beloved Son."

Colossians 1:13

"This is the message we have heard from him and proclaim to
you, that God is light and in him is no darkness at all."

1 John 1:5

My spiritual awakening began in 1971 when I moved away from home to attend the University of Puget Sound in Tacoma, Washington. After I was free from the oppression, I grew about five inches the next year and I began to excel at school, earning a 3.75 GPA in the first semester. I had been told that I was a failure at math, but I received an A in my first college mathematics course. I scored one hundred percent on several tests and the teacher encouraged me to seek a degree in mathematics. Once I escaped the negativity, I discovered that I was not a failure. I earned a Bachelor's degree in business and history. I liked history because I could study how God had influenced the events that have occurred on this earth, and I chose business because I planned to start my own company after I graduated. With the Lord's help, in four years I was two classes short of my third Bachelor's degree in economics. These majors were acceptable to my dictator mother as long as I went to law school. I was young and I made a poor decision to join a fraternity. I did not like drinking, doing drugs, or partying, but these were required activities to stay in the program. While the rest of the members consumed an insane amount of alcohol and drugs, I spent the night with an empty cup and acted drunk so that they would not kick me out. They literally filled a plastic swimming pool with liquor and sucked the alcohol out with tubes. During one party, I made the mistake of trying the punch and I was almost blinded by the "white lightning" (pure alcohol). I did not understand why people choose to live in this kind of environment. One night, I attempted to get up to my top bunk and I slipped on someone's beer bottle and broke my wrist. The fraternity photo at the end of that first year included me laying in front of the members with a cast on my arm. The fraternity had bizarre initiation activities such as dragging naked pledges on the grass around the school. Occasionally, there were violent battles against the other fraternities that resulted in arrests and criminal charges. I was glad to leave that fraternity and I continued to search for the true Jesus and the true Church.

When I was twenty-one years old, the Father revealed Himself to me as the Creator of all things as I hiked across the mountains of Switzerland. The Lord gave me a vision of the new heaven and earth, and this trip was the most amazing experience of my life. My father

The earth is the LORD'S, and the fulness thereof, the world and all those who dwell therein. **Psalm 24.1**

This photograph was taken in Rosenlaui on my hiking trip through Switzerland

helped me ship my motorcycle to Switzerland, but it was detained in customs for three weeks because this was the first time that a Honda 550 had been "imported" into the country. The Swiss government has a complex bureaucracy and they forced us to modify the motorcycle. For example, they changed the rubber spark plug cover to a metal one which caused a periodic short in the ignition system for the remainder of the trip. While this bureaucratic nightmare was occurring, my friend and I took a train up to Meiringen and started our three-week hiking trip across the Bernese Oberland mountains. We walked up to Rosenlaui to see the Wetterhorn and then on to Grindelwald to view the Eiger. During the three-week hike, I would periodically call the customs agent and his response was always, "not good, not good." The enemy was trying to stop the trip, but God was working in all of it for good and the three-week hiking trip was the highlight of my entire trip to Europe. I continued on my journey to Wengen and Murren as I viewed the spectacular Monch and the Jungfrau mountains. We usually camped in a tent, but occasionally we stayed in hiking cabins in the mountains. This was a low-budget trip and I don't remember staying in a hotel for the entire two months. We spent about $1700 for the entire trip, which included shipping the bike. Several times, I chose to walk several miles up a road to save the fifty-cent bus fare. As I hiked, the Lord showed me an amazing vision of the new heaven and earth and I was surrounded by His glory that was shining out of the mountains, hills, fields, and flowers. It seemed that I had stepped into heaven. The Lord revealed to me several years later that the times that I walked with Him in the mountains were in heavenly places and not on this earth. These visions of God's glory gave me hope through many difficult years of suffering. As I walked across Switzerland, I was in awe of His majesty that seemed to fill all my senses. God's Word declares that in heaven, we will no longer need the light of the sun, moon, or lamp because His glory will be our light. (Revelation 21:22–23). I was surrounded by His glory that filled the mountains, valleys, trees, clouds, and even the houses. I experienced incredible joy in the presence of God and my only desire was to spend eternity with Him. In Switzerland, the Lord revealed to me that in the next life, the Church will live in glorious mansions in perfect harmony with God's beautiful creation. Several years later, the Father showed me a vision of the mansion that He has prepared for me in heaven. The house will be almost a "V" shape (but more flattened) with a fireplace in the middle and large windows. There will be a small creek in front of the house and the land will look similar to the property that my father had promised to give me (see the photograph in chapter seven). The Lord helped me design the house and the shape is difficult to describe with words—but it will be glorious. Jesus will soon come and take us to mansions in a beautiful new land that is waiting for us in heaven (John 14:1-3). It is difficult to explain the joy of having every part of my being alive in His presence. God's love and goodness were in me, around me, and in all creation. I saw beauty and glory that was far beyond anything I could have ever imagined. I prayed, "Oh, let me dwell in Thy house forever singing Thy praise. This is all I ask of Thee. I am a sinner and I don't deserve such a reward, but in Thy grace and mercy, let me dwell close to your heart forever." In this world, we will have tribulations, but we set our hope on the reward of spending eternity in God's glorious presence. Like Enoch, I will seek to walk each day with God by faith, with the hope that one day I will see Him face-to-face (Genesis 5:22–24). During this time, the Holy Spirit began to reveal the indescribable reward that God has prepared for us: "'What no eye has seen, nor ear heard, nor the heart of man conceived, what God has prepared for those who love Him, God has revealed to us through the Spirit'" (1 Corinthians 2:9–10). At the time, I did not realize that this trip would be one of the highlights of my entire life.

After three weeks of hiking, I was able to obtain my motorcycle from customs and I rode around the entire country of Switzerland. I traveled through many beautiful mountains surrounded by glaciers and I was astonished at the engineering required to build these roads over these high mountain passes. I rode to Zermatt and skied in July on an eleven-thousand-foot glacier near the foot of the Matterhorn. My father met me in Zermatt and he said, "it looked like I grew out of the mountains or the mountains grew out of me." I also traveled through the beautiful countryside of France, and the scenery reminded me of my favorite painter, Vincent van Gogh. I explored the beautiful French Alps at Chamonix and I rode on a gondola up to twelve thousand feet to view the amazing area around Mount Blanc.

My friend and I camped in inexpensive campgrounds that usually cost about two dollars a night (I'm sure that they cost more now). Europe is unique because there are good campgrounds in almost every city. In England, I initially had difficulty adjusting to driving on the opposite side of the road. On one of my first days riding in England, I went the wrong direction around a roundabout. I was heading toward the oncoming traffic until a man came out of the fire station waving his hands and warned me to turn around. He told me that the cover of the Beatles album "Abbey Road" was filmed at this intersection. I met some amazing people on my trip. In London, I stayed with a man who lived in a "flat" at the top of a tower. He informed me that he received a discount in rent because the two other towers built at the same time had already collapsed. He said, "at least I will be at the top of the rubble if his building falls down." One day, he pointed out of his window at a policeman shooting at a criminal and he stated, "see, it is just like America." I tried to explain to him that our country is not like the movies. He was proud that he drank at a pub that was built before America became a country. I traveled up through Germany and Denmark to Bergen, Norway, where my ancestors had previously lived. My great-grandfather was a sea captain and his family lived alone on a remote island in the North

Blessed is he whom Thou dost choose and bring near, to dwell in Thy courts! Psam 65.4

Zermatt and the Matterhorn. I skied at the foot of this mountain.

Atlantic. The children rowed to school every day in a small boat. I explored many amazing fjords and camped at the beautiful lake Tyin. The first photograph in this book is the view of this lake from our campsite. During this time, I was also blessed to ride my motorcycle from Idaho to Glacier National Park in Montana and finally to Banff, Lake Louise, and Jasper in Canada. I traveled over many high mountain passes and camped on meadows beside rivers and lakes. God's creation is so beautiful!

After this glorious trip, I returned to college and joined a climbing class. The instructor was reckless, and on one climbing trip, he told me to lead the class across an obvious avalanche field. A couple of weeks later, the class was scheduled to climb Mount Saint Helens, but I was warned by the Spirit not to join the trip (this was several years before the mountain erupted). On the trip, the entire class was caught in an avalanche while sleeping in their tents and seven students died. I believe that there was a tremor inside the mountain that set off the avalanche. The Lord had saved my life—thank you, Jesus. The instructor continued to teach the class and asked me to lead another climb, but I declined. I graduated from the university and I was forced by my mother to go to law school or face being disowned. I had a difficult time at the University of Puget Sound Law School because I was afraid of speaking in front of people due to childhood abuse. The professors used the Socratic method of teaching and they would randomly call on students to test their knowledge of the law and their ability to speak. I lived in constant fear of being called on to answer these legal questions. I remained socially isolated in school and I did not enjoy reading thousands of pages of boring legal opinions. I came home several times to inform my mother that I was quitting, but I changed my mind after she threatened to throw me out on the street. I persevered through three miserable years of night school until Jesus moved me to Idaho. The Lord was already beginning to set me free from the oppression and I became a top student and athlete. I excelled in skiing, hiking, mountain climbing, bike riding, and cross-country skiing. Jesus would soon reveal Himself to me as my risen Lord and Savior.

3

Spiritual Awakening

"And I will pray to the Father, and he will give you another
Counselor, to be with you forever."

John 14:18

"But you shall receive power when the Holy Spirit has come
upon you; and you shall be my witnesses in Jerusalem and in
all Judea and Samaria and to the end of the earth."

Acts 1:8

In 1975, I saw the glory of the risen Christ when I was invited to
a Charismatic Church. I gave my life to Christ and for the next
three and a half years I walked in the amazing anointing similar
to what was experienced by the early Church. The Father spoke to
me, "Awake O sleeper, and arise from the dead, and Christ shall give
you light" (Ephesians 5:14). Jesus revealed to me that I had been
asleep in sin and darkness and that He had sent His Spirit into me
to raise me from the dead. I was now born again by the Holy Spirit
and Jesus began to unveil His plan and purpose for my life. I tasted
the goodness of the Lord and worshiped Him with all my heart. His
presence filled my heart and I finally understood that Jesus has risen
and that He reigns in the hearts of His believers. I walked in great

joy in the Spirit that no one could take away. I loved everyone, and most of all, I loved the Lord. I stood in awe of His anointing and His glory in the Church. I found the joy of God's presence and fellowship with other Spirit-filled believers. During this time, I was baptized in the Holy Spirit. A brother from the Church asked me if I had been filled with the Spirit and I replied that I had never heard of Pentecost, baptism of the Spirit, or speaking in tongues. I had not been taught the truth about the promise of the Holy Spirit in the dead Churches of my childhood. We read the first several verses of Acts chapter 2, and I was filled with the Holy Spirit and began to speak in tongues. The power of God came upon me as in the days of the early Church and changed my life. The Word of God is clear that the baptism of the Holy Spirit was not just for the early Church, but for all subsequent generations. The promise of the Spirit is for everyone whom the Lord calls unto Himself (Acts 2: 38-39). I have decided not to live in fear and doubt, but to receive every gift that the Holy Spirit wants to give me. Through the Holy Spirit, I received the power of Christ to lay down my life and then the power to be raised with Him (John 10:18). After my baptism, I was filled with the immeasurable resurrection power of Christ to obey the Father (Acts 1:8). Thank you, Jesus! Every good and perfect gift comes from the Father (James 1:17).

I experienced the true joy of fellowship in the Holy Spirit as I attended this Charismatic Church several times a week. The worship was so powerful that we would often sing in spiritual tongues for ten or fifteen minutes between every song. I saw the Bride of Christ all turned to Him in worship as each member would praise Jesus in their own words. We stood in awe of Jesus, and every day was a blessed gift from God. I walked in the Spirit and I required only four hours of sleep each night—from 2 a.m. to 6 a.m. I ate very little in those days, and my dinners often consisted of two hot dogs and macaroni and cheese. This was a time of great spiritual blessings and I saw miracles that resembled those in the early Church. Demons were cast out of people while they were sitting in the pews. Jesus spoke to us through His Spirit, and we loved Him with all our hearts. I attended law school between 6 p.m. and 10 p.m. at night and enjoyed Bible school during the day. I sat at His feet as He taught me His holy Word. We studied the books of Acts, Romans, and Hebrews, and the Holy Spirit would speak through the teacher straight into my heart. I was so overcome with conviction and revelation that I was often unable to get up out of my seat for about ten minutes after the classes. As the Holy Spirit began to shine light into the darkness inside of me, I was convicted of my sin and cried out for Jesus to forgive me. I prayed for the Lord to remove anything in me that was not of Him. I asked Him to cleanse this temple and make me more like Christ. Jesus began to put a passion in me to know Him and I was filled with unspeakable joy. I will always thank the Lord for His incredible grace to allow me to see this Church filled with His glory. This was the most beautiful Church fellowship that I have ever experienced. Those years were truly a taste of heaven when we will be united with all believers from every age.

At this time, the Lord appeared to me in glory and the Father unveiled His plan for my life. For most of my life, I had often felt unworthy and unwanted, but the Lord was about to reveal to me that I was chosen by Him. While I was driving to Church on a Wednesday night, I was called by the Lord. Suddenly, I was in the Shekinah

On the glorious splendor of Thy majesty, and on Thy wondrous works will I meditate. Psalm 145.5

I envision myself in heaven, talking with the Lord as I view the Eiger, Monch, and Jungfrau mountains.

Glory of God. I looked up and saw hundreds of angels in circular ascending balconies stretching up to heaven. The Lord told me to take off my shoes because I was standing on holy ground. He spoke to me: "Thou art My chosen one," "Thou shalt bless all the nations," and, "I am God". He also crippled my hands and then healed them several minutes later as a sign that He would soon take away my life and then give it back to me. I had been called to suffer for Christ, and this seven-year season of suffering began in 1981. The presence of the Lord was so amazing that my deepest desire was to walk in fellowship with Him for the rest of my life. Later in the evening, I came to Church filled with joy, and many commented that I was still glowing with God's glory. The joy was so intense that I had difficulty sitting still in the pew. The first song that we sang began with the words, "I saw the Lord; He was high and lifted up and His train filled the temple" (Isaiah 6:1). Thank you, Father, for Your amazing grace!

I met my first wife at this Church and we were married about two years later. She was an amazing prophet, and she wrote many visions and prophecies to prepare me for this time of suffering. She had been classified as seriously mentally ill, but she stopped taking her medication because she believed that she was healed. After two years, we were married and we rented a house in Tacoma, Washington until the Lord called us to move to Idaho. The Holy Spirit began to teach me about the Cross and the purpose of suffering. The Lord would soon lead me into the wilderness to overcome the power of the flesh, sin, and the enemy (Luke 4:1–12). The Lord planned to prepare me for ministry by baptizing me with fire to burn away anything that was not of Him (Luke 3:16). God would soon discipline me to give me victory over my sinful nature (Hebrews 12:5–11). I asked the Lord to remove anything in me that was not of Him so that I might know Him (Philippians 3:7–11). I will always remember those glorious years when I walked in the anointing of the Holy Spirit. God had given me a taste of His presence that would give me hope during the dark days to come. Taste and see that the Lord is good! (Psalm 34:8).

4

Idaho: My Promised Land

"But according to his promise we wait for a new heaven and a
new earth in which righteousness dwells."

2 Peter 3:13

"Your eyes will see the king in his beauty, they will behold a
land that stretches afar."

Isaiah 33:17

For many years, Idaho was my "promised land" where I could seek God and escape the oppression and darkness of my childhood. The Lord was merciful to me and He allowed me to experience some wonderful times with my father in the mountains of Idaho. As I am writing this account, I feel his presence in a very strong way and I am reminded of the amazing adventures that we experienced together in Idaho. When I was ten years old, my father started taking the family on vacations to Sun Valley Idaho. I enjoyed skiing, sleigh rides, cross-country skiing in the winter, and exploring this beautiful country by hiking and riding my dirt bike in the summer. When I was young, Sun Valley seemed like a wonderful and enchanted playground. My dad eventually built a vacation home near the ski mountain for us to enjoy. My father and I especially loved motorcycle riding together, and we would travel hundreds of miles on dirt roads and trails over high mountain passes and across many beautiful valleys. My father and I would also hike through meadows filled with flowers and up to many beautiful lakes. The land was young and still uncrowded and we often felt like the early pioneers exploring the land for the first time. We both loved God, and we enjoyed exploring this beautiful land together. I am thankful to have spent these wonderful times hiking, fishing, and riding motorcycles with my dad. I am more like my father than anyone else that I have met in this life. When I was twenty-six years old, the Lord took him home when he was riding his motorcycle in Idaho. After he died, I explored this earth alone with my heavenly Father—I never found anyone that loved God's creation in the same way, and he will be the first person I will look for in heaven.

I often think of the joy I experienced in fellowship with the Lord as I skied down the mountain and carved turns in the velvet snow. My passion was to ski with all my heart and strength. I loved the beauty of the white snow and the deep blue skies, and I wanted to ski forever. I enjoyed ski runs like College, Warm Springs, Flying Squirrel, and Grayhawk. I loved making quick slalom turns at a high rate of speed. The Lord has been good to me and He gave me the gift to ski. Sometimes, people would cheer on the chairlifts as I came down the mountain. One day, two professional skiers on the chairlift applauded me as I skied by them. One of the men said, "nice skis" because he was sponsored by the company that made my skis. It is all by the grace of God, all glory goes to Him. When the new snow fell, I was in line before the lifts opened to make the first turns in the fresh snow. Many times, I would reach the bottom of the ski hill with my arms raised in pure joy. I loved skiing with all my heart and at the end of the day, I was often too exhausted to move. One day, I skied during a total eclipse, and in the darkness, I fell backward off a cliff—fortunately, I was not injured. During snowstorms, there were often "whiteouts" where I couldn't see. Another time, I followed a group of three people on a trail at the top of the mountain in zero visibility. I heard the leader of the group say to his two friends, "I'm sure glad I know where I am going." Immediately, all three skied off a cliff and completely disappeared (they were not injured). I thought of the story that Jesus told His disciples, "And if a blind man leads a blind man, both will fall into a pit" (Matthew 15:14). When new snow fell, I skied in some dangerous areas with large cliffs and I had several spectacular falls. The snow was sometimes so deep that it was difficult to breathe, and I considered using a snorkel. One day, I skied on the side of a run and a hidden stick tore a hole in my hip. I went directly to the medical clinic and I informed the staff that I was bleeding. They told me to "sit down and wait my turn," but a few minutes later they realized I was bleeding on the chairs and they rushed me in to perform surgery. I still have a six-inch scar from that injury. I often enjoyed sitting in the hot tub in below-zero temperatures. I would frequently leap out of the tub and run through the snow to jump into the extremely cold river. I would then run back to the tub with bright red skin from the cold temperatures. I also enjoyed hiking up mountains in the backcountry and then skiing down the other side. During those precious times, He raised me above the darkness of this earth and held me in His arms. I will carry the memory of those days in my heart forever, and I am grateful for His blessings. I no longer ski on this earth, but I believe that God has prepared a place for me in the next life where I will ski in the presence of the Lord. Those wonderful days were truly a gift from God, and I will always be thankful for all those amazing years I spent skiing in fellowship with the Lord. Thank you, Jesus!

For many years, I hiked up to the top of mountains in Idaho to escape the darkness of this world and spend time with the Father. I climbed up to the highest peaks and He often spoke to me as a friend. I wanted to stay up there with Him forever, just as Peter did on the Mount of Transfiguration (Luke 9:28–36). Many times, I climbed up to the Pioneer Mountains in Idaho and spent the day with the Lord, often surrounded by several mountain goats. He made my legs strong and agile so I could tread upon His high places. "God, the Lord, is

The heavens are telling the glory of God; and the firmament proclaims His handiwork.
Psalm 19.1

Warm Springs valley in winter near Sun Valley Idaho

my strength; He makes my feet like hind's feet, He makes me tread upon my high places" (Habakkuk 3:19). The Lord gave me the amazing strength to hike up to twenty miles in a day. One day in the Pioneer mountains, I climbed to a ridge and there was a mountain goat nearby who helped lead me up to the top of a 12,000-foot peak, which was the highest in the area. Most of the time, I hiked off the trail and explored many hidden and beautiful areas. I also climbed Cobb Peak and several other mountains in this Pioneer Range. I didn't need a map or a trail—I would see a ridge or a mountain and climb up to it. It often seemed that I was the first person to explore these beautiful places. I walked through forests and discovered hidden meadows full of beautiful flowers. The Father is so amazing—I climbed His shining mountains and I looked down upon the golden valleys. I hiked up high mountain passes in the Sawtooth Mountains and viewed His majesty. One day while walking near Sawtooth lake, I saw a vision of Jesus in a white robe. On the way back, the hikers who passed by me looked shocked because they could see the glory of God on my face. I often traveled on a boat to the end of Redfish Lake and then hiked to Shangrila Lakes and Baron Pass. I walked in heavenly places, and I beheld His glory. I loved Him and I loved His creation. God gave me the grace to climb to the highest peaks above the darkness below. I often hiked to high places in the Lost River Range and I was in awe of His beautiful creation. One of my favorite areas was the Pashimerio Valley, and I frequently climbed to the top of a mountain to talk with God. Many times, I carried an extra container of gas and then traveled over one hundred miles around the Lost River Range.

For My mountains may depart and the hills be removed, but My steadfast love shall not depart from you. Isaiah 54.10

One of my favorite places in Idaho is the Pahsimeroi Valley in the Lost River Range. I climbed to the top of the smaller mountain on the right and spent the day talking with God.

When I was in God's presence, the wild animals were not afraid of me. I was able to hike with the animals and sometimes touch them. I remember holding onto the velvet antlers of a deer and playing "tug of war" with him. I spent many years exploring the Father's beautiful creation with deer, elk, antelope, moose, mountain goats, bighorn sheep, black bears, mountain lions, and even wolverines. One day, a porcupine came up to me and wanted to be petted. I had to explain to him that I could not pick him up because of his sharp spines. I would often walk alone through the forests and see a herd of elk grazing in a meadow with flowers. One day, I hiked with a mountain goat in Glacier National Park. A hiker yelled at me for "harming the goat" and her angry voice caused him to run away. The Father revealed to me that in the next life, we will live in perfect harmony with all of God's creatures. Every spring, I rode my motorcycle to Cooper Basin, and I often raced the antelope that ran beside me at about forty-five miles per hour. I would eventually slow down to about forty miles per hour, and they would cross in front of my motorcycle to boast that they were faster than me. During one of these trips, I rode across a stream and ran into a rock wall. The water caused the engine to stop, and my dad helped me "compression start" my bike. One summer, I was riding on a dirt road a couple of miles from home and the police stopped me and ordered me to walk the bike back the two miles to my house. Instead, I drove home down a nearby stream, and the water in the stream was occasionally higher than the seat. The Lord protected me from harm when a grizzly came into our camp near Lake Louise in Canada. I foolishly went to the same area where a grizzly had mauled a woman the previous day, and I endured several stressful hours in my tent listening to the bear eat food and destroy the camp. I laid on my stomach as I had been taught by the rangers (so if the bear attacked me, it would not damage my internal organs). Fortunately, a pack train with horses came by early in the morning and chased the bear away. What a privilege it was to be invited to see God's glory and talk with Him on those mountains. I am eternally grateful for everything that He has given me. I am a sinner, but He loved me anyway. He was pleased with my heart, and I found favor in His sight. He allowed me to know Him—what a wonderful gift. Through Christ, I am His son and He is my Father.

5

Joy in the Mountains of Idaho

"One thing have I asked of the LORD, that will I seek after,
that I may dwell in the house of the LORD all the days of
my life, to behold the beauty of the LORD, and to inquire in
his temple."

Psalms 27:4

"Thou dost show me the path of life, in thy presence there is
fulness of joy, in thy right hand are pleasures for evermore."
(Psalms 16"11).

After my father died, I spent many wonderful years walking with my heavenly Father and exploring the beautiful area around Sun Valley. The land was young and green, and I was safe because God was with me. One of my favorite places to meet with God was at the top of Corral Creek Summit overlooking the Lost River Range. Many times, I rode my dirt bike over Trail Creek Summit and then explored every road and trail I could find. I saw His glory, and I was content with the goodness of the Lord. I loved His creation and His creatures, but most of all, I loved Him. One day, I was riding around a bend near Dollarhide summit and two mountain lions were standing in the road. They were so frightened that they sprang up about six feet off the ground and quickly ran away. I went up many mountain passes and through fields of flowers with the wind on my face. Several times, I rode my bike up steep trails to a fire lookout on top of Soldier mountain. The Lord protected me as I traveled alone on narrow trails where one mistake would mean death or serious injury—I was never afraid because the Lord was always with me. I beheld God's beauty and I viewed a land untouched by the sinfulness of man. In the spring, I rode my bike on snow-covered trails and I occasionally encountered deep snowfields. I accelerated my bike to a high rate of speed and attempted to slide over the snowbank. Several times, I sank deep into the snow and with great difficulty, I was able to dig out the bike and push it to safety.

I also rode my mountain bicycle on many trails with names such as Greenhorn Gulch, Adams Gulch, Deer Creek, Stairway to Heaven, Fourth of July Creek, and Corral Creek. The Father gave me the strength to climb up steep trails and go up to His high places. I felt as free as the wind as I rode down these paths moving side to side with every turn. I enjoyed many steep and challenging trails in the Pioneer, White Cloud, and Sawtooth mountains. Many times, I rode on my road bicycle for about fifty miles alongside the Boulder mountains—I loved it all. Truly, it was all good because it came from Him. The Father has given me perfect gifts through Jesus. The Lord blessed me with the ability to explore His creation and I was satisfied with His goodness. I sought Him with all my heart and He was always with me. Thank you, Lord! God has created so much beauty for us to enjoy! I have looked up to the stars and saw the expanse of His universe. How awesome and diverse is His creation! How amazing is His handiwork! "The heavens are telling the glory of God; and the firmament proclaims his handiwork" (Psalms 19:1). In this life, we see

Him through a dark mirror, and we are now able to experience only a taste of His glory. Even a taste of God's glory is amazing! I will spend eternity seeking to know more of God and exploring His beautiful new creation. I can only fall down and worship Him. I am in awe of all that He is and all that He has done.

I often experienced solitude with the Father as I enjoyed cross-country skiing in the Sawtooth Mountains of Idaho. I skied across the beautiful snow and through the forests for many miles. I frequently skated with my skis across great frozen lakes in the early spring. I was alone with God, and several times, the ice began to crack and I quickly skied to the shore. The Lord protected me from falling into the freezing water, which would have resulted in certain death. The air was cold, and the snow was white and pure. I found peace and joy gliding across the ice and snow with the clear blue skies. I thought of His eternal nature—endless and holy. He is pure and unstained by this present darkness. The world doesn't know the Father, but He has chosen to reveal Himself to those who believe. I am a sinner, but The Lord sees me in the righteousness and holiness of Christ. I am pure and white in His eyes, like the snow that I often skied across. By grace, He accepts me without condemnation, and He is pleased with my heart. I cleave to Christ in faith and nothing can separate me from His love. I come before Him in reverence and awe, and yet without fear because I am safe in His arms and He is always with me. The Father taught me to rest in His presence as I fly-fished on the Warm Springs, Big Wood, and Lost rivers in Idaho. I felt solitude and peace as I spent many days fishing for rainbow trout on peaceful streams surrounded by cottonwood trees and beautiful mountains. I rested in the presence of the Lord as I walked these beautiful streams.

I left behind the stress and worry of this life, and I ran after Him as a son runs after his father. I wanted to be with Him, to be like Him, and to hear His voice. When the evil of this world sought to pull me away from Christ, I escaped the darkness to spend time with Jesus. I laid down my burdens and worries at His feet, and He was faithful to take them from me and restore them. "In peace I will both lie down and sleep; for thou alone, O Lord, makest me dwell in safety" (Psalm 4:8). I am with my Heavenly Father, and all is well!

Then Jesus told his disciples, "If any man would come after me, let him deny himself and take up his cross and follow me.
Matthew 16.24

6

Suffering in the Mountains

"In this world you have tribulation, but be of good cheer, I
have overcome the world."

John 16:33

"For to this you have been called, because Christ also suffered
for you, leaving you an example, that you should follow in
his steps."

1 Peter 2:21

"Weeping may tarry for the night, but joy comes with
the morning."

Psalms 30:5

"They said to one another, 'Here comes this dreamer. Come
now, let us kill him and throw him into one of the pits; then
we shall say that a wild beast has devoured him, and we shall
see what will become of his dreams.'"

Genesis: 17:19

Idaho was a source of amazing joy to me, but also a place of great suffering. The Lord put me through this seven-year fire to refine me and prepare me to minister to the homeless for twenty-five years and then to fulfill His call on my life to preach the Gospel to the world. I had dreamed of living in Idaho for many years, and I was thankful when Jesus called me to move to Sun Valley in 1979. My goal was to start a landscaping business, explore the beautiful mountains and begin my new life with my wife. During this time, the Lord revealed to me that He had called me to suffer and for this reason, He did not want me to have children (although I have many "spiritual children"). I started installing landscaping for several large houses in the area, but in the spring of 1981, my leg swelled out to twice its size. I went to the doctor and he said that, " I could go to the hospital but it would be a waste of money because I would probably be dead the next day." I was near death for the next seven years as my liver and kidneys shut down and I swelled to about five hundred pounds with yellow jaundice fluid. My body was filled with the poisons that a healthy liver and kidney normally expel every day. My digestive system stopped working and the food passed through me undigested. My stomach swelled out to about twice its size and I was concerned that it would burst. I had no digestive enzymes and I often chewed the same piece of food for hours. My hair turned gray and fell out at the age of twenty-seven. I could sleep only a couple of hours a week and I lived during the night. The pain was so intense that I would only face it one second at a time—I did not have the strength to think about the future pain. Jesus kept me alive and carried me through the most difficult times. The poisons erased my memory—I had two college degrees but I no longer knew that two-plus-two-equals-four. I was too weak to read even one line on a page. I had been a top athlete, but for seven years I could only walk a couple of feet at a time. My favorite activity had been skiing, but I no longer remembered that I was a skier. I lived at night and I traveled to town through an extremely unreliable bus service. I often waited at bus stops for two to three hours in below-zero temperatures with a size medium jacket that did not fit my five hundred pound body. The local newspaper posted a cartoon of a skeleton waiting on a bench for the bus, and I felt like this cartoon was describing my situation. The buses were in terrible mechanical condition and one night, the steering wheel fell off while we were driving into town. On New Year's Eve one year, the bus driver was so drunk that the police stopped the bus and arrested him. Looking back on these years, I am amazed that I was able to walk with the Lord while suffering from severe physical and mental illness and complete memory loss. Jesus was all I remembered and all I needed. I received no human support, so the Lord provided heavenly assistance through the cloud of witnesses (the saints who have died in Christ in previous generations). For example, they would make a way for someone to buy a ten-dollar item so that I could eat that day. Thank you, Jesus. I was dead in the flesh and alive in the Spirit, and I began to see the spiritual realm that is usually hidden beyond the veil. Like John in the book of Revelation, I saw the spiritual battle between Jesus and his angels and the devil and his demons. The Lord gave me amazing revelations from the books of Daniel, Ezekiel, Zechariah, and Revelation. I was taught by the Holy Spirit and not from man's interpretations (Galatians 1:11,-2). The Spirit led me through each verse of Revelation and Daniel, and He taught me about the beast, the false prophet, the harlot, and the seven seals, seven trumpets, and seven bowls. The Lord gave me the spiritual understanding of Armageddon, Gog and Magog, the White Throne, and the New Jerusalem. The Lord showed me many revelations and visions that I can not share at this time. In the same way, Jesus gave Paul visions of paradise that he was not permitted to disclose on this earth (2 Corinthians 12:1-6). I walked in the Spirit through these end time prophecies in the Bible. Every day was filled with intense pain and amazing miracles. Often, these Biblical prophecies were connected with events in my life. For example, in 1983, the Lord was revealing to me the prophecy about the stone (Jesus) that struck the beast, and there was a 7.1 earthquake about forty miles away and it caused the Lost River range to rise over a foot and the valley to sink (Daniel 2:31-35) The fault line which stretched across the entire mountain range and springs of water opened up in the valley floor. On May 8th, 1980, I saw a snake on the ground and the Lord told me to kill it. Unknown to me, Mount Saint Helens had just exploded, which caused volcanic ash to spread over most of the world. I obeyed the Lord and killed the snake with a rock, and Sun Valley was one of the only places in the world that did not get any ash. The Holy Spirit revealed to me that Jesus is not coming back according to man's religious understanding. Two thousand years ago, the religious leaders did not recognize their own Messiah because they expected an earthly king and not a suffering servant who came to die for their sins. In the same way, Jesus is coming again in a way and at a time that we do not expect. The Scriptures teach that the faithful and wise servant of Christ is ready for His return, but the unfaithful servant will be punished. Are we ready for the coming of Jesus?

Peter Schuler

The Lord preserves all who love Him. Psalms 145.20

Lupines are one of my favorite wildflowers.

I spent seven years at the point of death with no money, while my family lived in luxury. My family often came to Sun Valley on vacations and occasionally they would see me barely alive on the street or in a store. They would laugh and call me "hippo Pete" with demonic voices and make jokes about my size. They mocked me by saying "poor Pete" and sarcastically talked about "love" as they looked at me with eyes of demonic hate. One night, I was so desperate after not eating for a week that I came to their house to ask for help. I knocked on their door, clothed in rags in below-zero temperatures, and they refused to feed me. They were eating an extravagant dinner (they boasted about the price of the food), and living in luxury in their beautiful vacation home, which they inherited from my father.

I was like a beggar on the street who was turned away by my own family. I mentioned that I used to be part of the family and I spoke of my room located on the lower floor. They denied that I was ever part of the family and stated that it has always been my brother's room. I was dying of starvation, and they would not share even a few scraps from their table. It was a very sad night, but Jesus carried me through the sorrow. I felt like the beggar named Lazarus in Luke chapter 16: "There was a rich man, who was clothed in purple and fine linen and who feasted sumptuously every day. And at his gate lay a poor man named Lazarus, full of sores, who desired to be fed with what fell from the rich man's table; moreover the dogs came and licked his sores. The poor man died and was carried by the angels to Abraham's bosom. The rich man also died and was buried" (Luke 16:19-22). The rich man was tormented in hell and he called out to Abraham for mercy, but he replied, "'Son, remember that you in your lifetime received your good things, and Lazarus in like manner evil things, but now he is comforted here, and you are in anguish'" (Luke 16:25). The wicked man was blessed by the devil in this life, while the believer who loved God suffered without mercy at his hands. In the next life, Lazarus was rewarded and the rich man was punished. The Bible teaches that there are righteous men to whom it happens according to the deeds of the wicked, and there are wicked men to whom it happens according to the deeds of the righteous (Ecclesiastes 8:14). My family also refused to notify me that my grandfather had left an inheritance about three years earlier. This money would have helped alleviate years of severe suffering. The State of Oregon had attempted to locate me for several years and made multiple inquiries to the entire family, but they declined to tell them where I was living.

They felt no compassion for me, although they knew I was extremely ill, starving, and near death. In contrast, I experienced amazing kindness and compassion on a trip through Montana several years later. I ran out of gas on the Blood Indian Reservation and one of the leaders of the six-thousand member tribe assisted me on the highway and then invited me to stay at his home for two and one half weeks. I told them about my seven-year illness, and they were appalled that I had not been offered any assistance during my illness. He informed me that on the reservation I would have been given money, land and a house. The man then met with the other leaders and attempted to obtain a house and land for me on the reservation. During the meeting, they spoke English for half their sentences and Blackfoot for the other half. Some of the older chiefs decided not to provide housing for me. I continued on my journey, but I will never forget their love and kindness. The next summer, members of the tribe did a cultural exchange with Sun Valley in an attempt to explain their culture to people who lived in the area. Eventually, God intervened and He made my family reveal my location to the State of Oregon. The arrival of the money signaled the beginning of the Lord's healing from the illness. The enemy had told them that they would be able to kill me, and they were shocked when Jesus raised me up and completely restored me. Three years ago, the Lord spoke to me. "You will rise, Peter, you will rise above them all," which was a promise that He will raise me above all the hate, rejection, and evil that I have experienced in this life.

Unfortunately, my wife lost her faith during this time of suffering. She was called to be a prophet, and she gave me many visions to help me through the seven-year illness. My wife was like Balaam the prophet who saw true prophecies, but fell away from God. Balaam had his eyes opened and saw true visions of God, but he did not truly believe and he perished (Numbers 24:4). Initially, my wife supported me during this time of suffering and intense spiritual warfare. After several years, she began to believe that the devil's power was stronger than God's. She was amazed at my mother's demonic power to change her height and weight. After several years, my wife decided that the devil was going to win the battle after witnessing the power of the enemy to torture me. Like Job's wife, she turned against me and joined the enemy. She moved to a city about seventy miles away and I brought her back home ten times. I did not believe in divorce until Jesus told me to let her go. One day, I stood at the door of my mobile home, and the Lord asked me to look inside. The trailer was filled to the ceiling with her things (she was a hoarder). She had taken over my mobile home and not one of my possessions were visible in my own home. The Lord warned me that if I didn't let her go, there would be nothing left of me. It was heartbreaking to lose my wife, but even more difficult because she had fallen away from God to join the enemy. I prayed for her eternal soul. The Lord told me that she had free will and that she had made her choice. In 1 Corinthians chapter seven, we are told to let the unbelieving spouse go if they choose to leave. She began to practice witchcraft and she gave me demonic "prophecies" that she would cripple me. About a year later, I was in an accident which caused my hip to be broken in twelve places. She also "prophesied" that she was planning to steal all my money, and in the next several years, tens of thousands of dollars were stolen by my friends and the homeless people that I was assisting. I took a friend with me to help pack her things after she had moved out of her apartment. He had previously been involved in witchcraft and he refused to go into the apartment because he sensed the evil in the home. My heart was torn in two when she left, but Jesus carried me through this difficult time and healed my heart. At the appointed time, the Spirit raised me up and Jesus healed me physically, mentally, and emotionally. The Lord restored my memory and healed the anger and bitterness in my heart. I was called to go back into this physical world, and I asked God to take away some of the ability to see the spiritual realm so that I could work and interact with people. The story of my illness and subsequent healing is explained in more detail in my books *In Pursuit of God A Love Story* and *Warrior for Christ: Overcoming Cancer by Faith.*

Thou dost show me the path of life; in Thy presence there is fulness of joy, in Thy right hand are pleasures for evermore.
Psalm 16.11

7

A Time of Healing in Idaho

"I believe that I shall see the goodness of the LORD in the land of the living!"

Psalms 27:13

"O LORD, thou hast brought up my soul from Sheol, restored me to life from among those gone down to the Pit."

Psalms 30:3

"He sent forth his word, and healed them, and delivered them from destruction."

Psalms 107:20

The Lord called me into a seven-year season of healing and restoration from my illness, and I began to ski, hike, climb mountains, ride my bicycle, and my dirt bike. I will always cherish this time of fellowship and intimacy with the Father. This was a taste of heaven where we will spend eternity in His glorious presence. These were some of the happiest times of my life as I enjoyed his beautiful creation in the area around Sun Valley. I restarted my landscaping company, but business was slow in the beginning, so I worked on several construction jobs to supplement my income. I did not enjoy this work because there was much substance abuse, anger, and foul language from my supervisors and co-workers. Thankfully, the Lord blessed my landscaping business, and I installed landscaping and maintained yards for many landowners in the area. They also hired me to do many other side jobs such as painting, construction cleanup, moving, and even a party rental business. The wealthy landowners were sometimes demanding and eccentric. I remember setting up a tent for a party rental business during a violent thunderstorm when lightning struck the field nearby. We were completely soaked and the owner of the business called me from her dry office and yelled at me "not to let anything get wet." There was not one thing dry in the whole area. For obvious reasons, that was my last day at the job. I was the first landscaper in the area to transplant forty-foot-tall spruce trees. I hired an owner of the tree spade company in Boise to bring the large spruce trees up to Sun Valley using a specifically designed semi-trailer to haul four trees at a time. He transported several loads of trees almost two hundred miles and planted them in the landowner's yard. I made a guarantee to the owner that the trees would live, so I prayed and God answered my prayer. The only tree that died was one that the owner killed by washing away the roots with a hose. The other landscapers in the area attempted to duplicate what I had accomplished, but all of their trees died. Thank you, Lord, for answering my prayer. This landowner owned a two-and-a-half-million-dollar mansion on a beautiful stream, but he was devastated when his neighbor built a five-million-dollar home. His house was no longer the largest in the area, so he sold his home and moved away from the Sun Valley. Some landowners built their mansions as a monument to their success to impress their friends and neighbors.

There were many eccentric and wealthy people in the area, and one man built a two-million-dollar home and then tore it down and constructed a smaller one because his wife thought it was too big. One landowner built nine large garages to house hundreds of very expensive motorcycles. He stored millions of dollars in a large safe and paid me in one-hundred-dollar bills. I maintained a large property for an alcoholic man who had lost his family because of his addiction. He had multiple DUI's and the court required him to attend an alcohol treatment program. He asked me to housesit his home while he traveled down to Boise to a four-hundred-dollar-a-day substance abuse program. Despite my objections, he drove nearly two hundred miles with a glass and a full wine bottle. He arrived drunk at the center and taught a class on how to stop drinking. I inquired about his behavior and he replied that "he had been to so many programs and he could teach them better than the staff." He could teach it but he could not do it. Several times, he passed out drunk on the tile floor and he would look up at me and say, "leave me here and I will be able to get up in the morning." He was six-foot-five and too heavy for me to lift. I enjoyed staying in his house and sitting in the hot tub overlooking the river. He said to me several times, "you are nice, I hate nice." One evening, he fired me because he thought one of my workers was a drug addict. As an alcoholic, he said, "I hate drug addicts." I packed up and went home to my mobile home. I was content living in my small trailer because God's beautiful creation was all around me.

For several years, I did tree-trimming and removal with a friend who owned a bucket truck with a forty-foot lift. We removed many large one-hundred-foot trees that grew over the roofs of expensive houses. My friend used chains to catch the branches so that they didn't damage the roof. I enjoyed the challenge of trimming and removing these large trees for these landowners. One day, my friend was working on another job, and a tree flattened the cab of his truck. He drove the truck by looking out of a six-inch opening in the collapsed cab. He was stopped by the police, but they let him go after he explained the situation. He went to a nearby high school welding shop where they cut off the top of the cab, and he used the truck as a convertible until he could repair it. In the spring, the melting snow caused the rivers to rise, and I was often hired to place sandbags along the riverfront of several properties to protect the houses. One day, a news crew from Boise filmed us placing the sandbags, and we were on the Idaho evening news. The news in Idaho was usually relaxing and my wife called it the "farm and garden report." I purchased a 1955 ten-wheel dump truck which I used to haul dirt, gravel, and logs. One fall, I was up in the Boulder mountains cutting wood, and a tree fell on the steel walls of the dump truck bed. The bottom end of the tree struck me and threw me about ten feet. Another time, a tree almost crushed me and it damaged my back. I suffered through both of those injuries without medical attention because I lacked health insurance. I purchased three older trucks, but I sold them because I did not have the mechanical expertise to keep them running. I also purchased a motorized pipe puller and installed many sprinkler systems. I lived at six-thousand-feet and the winter temperatures at night were sometimes twenty-below-zero. For this reason, we were required to dig down six feet to connect to the waterline because the cold winter temperatures froze the ground. Every year, we also used air compressors to blow out the water in the lines. In the fall, I cut hundreds of cords of wood and I split the rounds using a cone-shaped wood splitter that I attached to the wheel of an old VW bug. I removed hundreds of dead one-hundred-foot cottonwoods and I then sold the firewood. I also laid thousands of square feet of sod, planted trees, flowers, and shrubs. I mowed many large lawns for the landowners—some were over an acre in size. Every day at work was an amazing adventure because I was surrounded by beautiful mountains and incredible animals. I often saw deer and even moose in the landowner's yards. The deer would get me into trouble with the landowners by eating the pansies and petunias that I had just planted. One day, a moose came into the yard where I was clearing brush and he began to feel trapped. The large moose looked angry and I sat in my pickup until he found a way back into the woods. I was also hired to remove beaver dams that were causing flooding to several houses in the area. I installed fountains, sandstone patios, pavers, and many walls using railroad ties and river rock. Every spring, I power raked the grass because the voles (not moles) would tunnel under the snow, eat a small portion of the grass and leave about ninety percent of the lawn to die. I often worked long hours, and one night, I used my pickup headlights to transplant over one hundred raspberry bushes. My friend and I replaced that roof on the local forest service building. This was our first roofing job, so we checked out several books from the local library. It was challenging work because we had to cover the roof with plastic every night to protect it from the snowstorms. My friend slipped on the plastic and fell off the roof, but fortunately, he was not injured. One year later, the forest service staff reported that there had been no leaks in the roof. I moved a landowner into a new house about eight miles away from his previous home. I hired several members of my Church and we transported five thirty-two-foot U-Haul truckloads of their possessions. The two children were spoiled and their toys filled one entire truck. They kept telling my helpers, "we hate you" and "we are praying that you die," and several of the workers did not return to help me the following day. Their mother liked bats and she released many of them on her property. I remember trying to brush something off of my ankle, and when I looked down it was a large black bat attached to my leg. They eventually moved to California and they paid me two hundred dollars to drive their convertible Porsche Targa to Sacramento. The husband said to me several times, "you should pay me to drive the Porsche." They were going to hire me to drive their Jeep Renegade to California but changed their minds when I asked whether I could visit Taos on the way down. Many clients owned exotic cars and one landowner parked two Ferraris in front of his home. I delivered firewood to Peter Cetera's home, who was the lead singer of the rock group Chicago. When I was told that the house was owned by "Peter Cetera from Chicago," I replied, " I am Peter Schuler from Seattle." I didn't realize until later what they were trying to tell me. I would clear the brush out of many yards and deliver about eighty large pickup loads to the dump every season. I worked for Adam West, who had played Batman in the TV series, and he climbed on top of my pickup to help me stack the load of brush. He would get upset when I accidentally called him Bruce (which was his character's name). The landfill started a new computer system which sent me a credit of almost a million dollars and I jokingly asked if I could cash in the balance of my account. The Lord poured out the windows of heaven for me, and the prosperity became so overwhelming that I prayed for it to slow down. I loved every minute of this time in Sun Valley. I lived in my mobile home, operated my landscaping business and, when the weather was good, I went up to the mountains to enjoy God's creation. After work, I often rode my bicycle for about twelve miles on a beautiful bike path near my home. In the winter, I did snow removal with my blower and shoveled the snow off of many roofs when the weight became too heavy. The snow load could damage the roof or injure people if it dropped onto the sidewalk. When the new snow fell, I completed my snow removal early in the morning and then lined up before the lift opened to enjoy the fresh powder. I would often arrive before nine a.m., even when the temperature was well below zero. The air was often so cold that the water in the air would freeze into beautiful ice crystals that sparkled in the sun. My breath would also freeze and my beard was often covered in icicles. In the spring, I enjoyed skiing on "corn snow" which was formed when the snow would melt in the day and then freeze at night. In March and April, I would often ski in the morning and do landscaping work in the afternoon. The snow depth where I lived was usually four to six feet deep in the winter. Living in the snow was sometimes challenging, and I spent many hours shoveling snow off of my walkway, roof, and vehicles. I burned firewood in my wood-burning stove during the cold winter nights and I installed an engine heater to warm up my pickup so that it would start in the morning. My vehicles were always four-wheel-drive trucks which helped me drive in the winter snow and navigate steep mountain roads in the summer. Sun Valley has some of the cleanest air in the continental US and I would often take walks at night to view the millions of stars and the Milky Way galaxy. One night, I saw a meteor burning across the sky which later landed in Montana. By contrast, during the great Yellowstone fire, the smoke was so thick that the sun was dark red during the middle of the day. I went on hiking trips during this time and the red sun looked surreal.

The fall was my favorite time of the year, and I have spent countless hours enjoying the yellow, orange, and red aspen and cottonwood trees. I will never forget the sun shining through these beautiful leaves with the clear fall skies above. I loved viewing the amazing "popcorn" white clouds against the deep blue sky. Every year, I traveled hundreds of miles on foot, bicycle, and motorcycle to see these brilliant fall colors. It was all so beautiful because the Lord is beautiful. The fall winds would blow and the leaves would fall on the meadows and streams, signaling that the winter snows would soon come. These were wonderful years of healing and restoration that helped me recover from the trauma of my seven-year illness. I walked with the Father, explored His magnificent creation, landscaped in the summer, and skied with all my heart in the winter. I loved living in the mountains of Idaho and I planned to stay in Sun Valley for the rest of my life. The Lord had different plans, and He called me to move to Phoenix and minister to the homeless. I am very thankful that the Lord allowed me to work for those seven years and enjoy the mountains. Truly, God is good.

After moving to Phoenix, I returned to Idaho the next summer to do landscaping work for a couple of months. God is good and He blessed me with enough income to pay my bills for the next year in Phoenix as I ministered to the homeless. During this time, I went on a missionary trip to Ghana, Africa, with the members of my Church in Idaho. The Holy Spirit moved gloriously and many were healed and brought to Christ. I spoke at several Churches and a refugee camp. I brought my guitar everywhere and I was often surrounded by beautiful children who sang and danced to the music. I had "instant friends" wherever I went. I visited an elementary school in a village, and the children were so well behaved that they seemed like angels. We also went to a high school and they stopped school so that the students could attend Church. I will always love the people that I met in Ghana. The next summer, I returned to Idaho to work with one of my friends from the homeless program. Unfortunately, I was in an accident, and my hip was broken in twelve places. The surgeon who performed the six-and-a-half-hour surgery warned me that I would probably be permanently disabled. Jesus carried me through the pain and completely healed me. The bill for my hospital stay was about thirty thousand dollars and I had no health insurance. The state catastrophic fund paid about sixteen thousand dollars, and I made arrangements to pay one thousand dollars a year until the remainder of the bill was paid in full.

I returned to Idaho for a three-week vacation in 2007 because I wanted to see the mountains one last time. I enjoyed my trip to Idaho, but it was apparent that the Holy Spirit had moved on to my ministry in the desert. I bought a used motorcycle (see the photograph below), traveled to all the familiar places, and talked to God on many mountain tops. I visited the piece of land on a creek that my father had promised to give me (he died before he was able to complete the gift). There had been a large fire in Idaho in the previous summer and the Sun Valley area was evacuated. I had learned about it on the news and I prayed for the protection of the land. God answers prayer—the huge fire stopped right at the edge of the property (in the photograph below, you can see a couple of burned trees in the right corner of the picture). On this trip, I hiked many trails, enjoyed fly fishing in the

Teach me Thy way,
O God that I may walk
in Thy truth; unite my
heart to fear Thy name.
Psalms 86.11

This is the motorcycle that I rode on my trip to Idaho with the Lost River Range in the background.
The photograph was taken on Corral Creek summit where I spent many hours talking with God.

streams, rode a bicycle, took photographs, and played my guitar to worship God. I enjoyed every minute of the trip, but it was time to move on and never look back. I have been very blessed in Phoenix with the anointing of the Spirit to minister to many needy people.

During the years that I have lived in Phoenix, I have continued to enjoy God's creation. I explored Arizona on my motorcycle, hiked many trails in Sedona, rode my bicycle on beautiful paths in Phoenix, and worshiped God with my guitar in several city parks. From 2008 to 2013, I spent my vacations in Utah exploring Zion National Park, Bryce Canyon, Capitol Reef, the Grand Canyon, Canyonlands, and

Let me dwell in Thy tent for ever! Oh to be safe under the shelter of Thy wings. Psalms 61.4

This is the land on Warm Springs creek that my father promised to give me, but he passed away before he could complete the gift.

Arches National Park. I traveled alone and spent the entire time with the Lord, praying, worshiping Him with my guitar, reading the Bible, and hiking through God's beautiful creation. I played beautiful worship music on my stereo as I drove on many amazing highways viewing God's magnificent scenery. I took many pictures on these trips and I have included some of them in this book. I traveled in October and November so that I could photograph the beautiful fall colors. Angel's landing was my favorite hiking trail in Zion National Park—the trail was very steep but the view was breathtaking. Often, I rented a bicycle and rode up the valley and then hiked the narrow canyon with the trees turning yellow, orange, and red. I enjoyed walking up the river to the Narrows Canyon where I was enclosed by amazing red and orange rock walls. Deer and wild turkeys often surrounded me as I played my guitar alongside the stream. In the higher sections of the park, I occasionally saw bighorn sheep. I traveled to Bryce Canyon and I viewed amazing rock formations called Hoodoos. I hiked on many incredible trails through narrow openings in the red, orange, and white sandstone rock formations. The fall colors were beautiful at the Capitol Reef park and I enjoyed viewing the many inspiring arches at the Arches National Park. My favorite trail was hiking up to Delicate Arch in the late afternoon to watch the sunset. In near darkness, I carefully walked down the steep path. One year, I traveled to Telluride, Colorado, to see the beautiful fall colors, and on the way back I drove through the beautiful Monument Valley. Every year, I stopped at the Grand Canyon and I enjoyed the solitude of the North Rim, but the South Rim was also very beautiful. I also traveled to the West entrance to view the spectacular Sky Walk overlooking the canyon. I am amazed at the Lord's kindness, that He graciously allowed me to enjoy these beautiful places. I traveled thousands of miles alone with the Lord, and He always protected me from harm. On my last two trips to Utah, my right hip and my back became so painful that I could only walk a couple of steps at a time. I did not realize it at the time, but cancer was already beginning to damage my back and hips. I thank God that I was able to take those trips before I became disabled. God is good!

GOD, the Lord,
is my strength;
he makes my feet
like hinds' feet,
He makes me tread
upon my high places.
Hab. 3.19

A Bighorn Sheep in Zion National Park in Utah

8

Ministry in Phoenix

"And he said to them, 'Follow me, and I will make you fishers of men.' Immediately, they left their nets and followed him.."

Matthew 4:19-20

"But I do not account my life of any value nor as precious to myself, if only I may accomplish my course and the ministry which I received from the Lord Jesus, to testify to the gospel of the grace of God."

Acts 20:24

In 1996, Jesus called me to move to Phoenix and minister to the homeless and those in jails and nursing homes. Recently, the Father revealed to me that my entire life has been preparation for me to fulfill His plan to preach the Gospel to many nations. In Sun Valley, the Lord began to give me a heart of compassion for the homeless. Jesus removed my hard, selfish heart and gave me His heart to love those in need. I remembered the years I had spent in poverty without assistance, and I wanted to help those who were suffering. During this time, I read Isaiah 58, which instructs us to bring the homeless into our homes to assist them. In obedience, I began to hire the homeless to do landscaping work, and I then invited them to stay in my small ten-by-fifty-five foot trailer. For the next two years, I filled my mobile home with homeless people who were in need. I hired one man and then provided shelter for his ex-wife and their two sons. The sixteen-year-old son stayed with me until he finished high school. He was very angry after being abandoned by both his parents. They called him "little Hitler" in high school because he would push people as he walked down the hallways of the facility. One of the teachers informed me that he was probably the most troubled child in the entire school. His mother had been on drugs during the pregnancy, which caused him to have brain damage. When he was eighteen, he stated, "I do love you, I haven't killed you or burned down your trailer." Apparently, this was the definition of love to a teenager who had been rejected by his family. The Lord put him in my life for a reason because twelve years later, he was standing next to me at the front desk of the shelter in Phoenix when I applied for a full-time position doing outreach to the homeless. I continued to help him for several years, and I was able to lead him to the Lord. In Idaho, I was inexperienced in working with the homeless and several of the men stole money from me. One man who was addicted to heroin put a large knife to my throat and stole my pickup and several thousand dollars. The father of the family that lived in my trailer observed that, "everyone who you have tried to help has stolen from you," The Scriptures tell us to joyfully accept the plundering of our property since we have a better and abiding possession in heaven (Hebrews 10:34). There is a cost to serving Jesus and ministering to those in need. Jesus was leading me into full-time ministry in Phoenix to teach me how to effectively minister to the homeless.

My pastor in Idaho asked me, "What if God called you to an inner-city ministry?" and I replied, "He would never do that because my life, home, and business are here in the mountains." I planned to spend the rest of my life in Sun Valley. I worked very hard and in seven years, I had saved up enough money for a down payment to buy a house in Bellevue, which was about thirteen miles south of Sun Valley. The service workers lived in this town because they were unable to afford the expensive houses near the ski resort. Jesus asked me how I could justify spending my money on this house when people were dying without Christ. By the grace of God, I obeyed the call of Jesus to give away my money and leave my home, business, and the beautiful mountains. I skied for my last time on the day that we left for Phoenix. My heart was torn in two when I left Sun Valley to obey the call of Jesus, but I will never regret this decision. I drove down to Phoenix with several members of my Church from Idaho, and I attended a pastor and leadership conference at a large Church in the area. The Church had a "Parade of Ministries" where they displayed several of their programs. I met several members of the homeless ministry, and the Lord called me to join them and stay in Phoenix. The members of my Church from Idaho were shocked when I stayed in Arizona because I had been very reluctant to go on the trip. It was a test of faith to leave everything behind and live at the homeless ministry located in the inner-city neighborhood which was surrounded by drug houses. Several years later, about ten ATF agents stormed the ministry because they thought it was a drug house (they arrested one of the residents for unpaid child support). I started attending the Church and I bought an inexpensive car at Jalopy Jungle. One night, the Holy Spirit anointed me for ministry while I sat in my car outside the Church. The Lord spoke to me, "The Spirit of the Lord is upon me because he has anointed me to preach good news to the poor. He has sent me to proclaim release to the captives and recovering of sight to the blind, to set at liberty those who are oppressed, to proclaim the acceptable year of the Lord." (Luke 4:18-19). The Father promised me several times that no person or spirit could ever stop this anointing. The Lord soon opened a door for me to teach a one-hour class at the ministry. I was very nervous because of my lifelong fear of speaking and singing in front of people. When I spoke, there seemed to be a large giant of fear trying to intimidate me. I stepped out by faith and completed the class. I had been called to preach, and God's strength is made perfect in weakness. All the glory goes to the Lord; I know that I am completely unable to do this ministry without Him. For the next twenty-five years, the Holy Spirit anointed me to preach, counsel, and lead worship services for thousands of people in eleven jails and prisons, four discipleship houses, three nursing homes, and on many street outreaches.

It has been a blessing to see the Holy Spirit move through me to touch many lives and bring many hundreds to Christ. In this ministry, I have seen hundreds of men and women filled with the Holy Spirit and a passion for God's Word in an age where many Christians are lukewarm and spiritually apathetic. Some of my jail services had a waiting list of over one hundred inmates. In one jail, I conducted four consecutive Church services, and so many inmates wanted to attend the meetings that the officers shut all of them down because it was a "violation of the fire code." In another jail, there was so much joy in a worship service that the officers stopped the meeting to determine what was happening. They were not sure what to do so they started a headcount, but in the middle of the procedure, the inmates started singing "This little light of mine," and the officers decided to let them continue. The head pastor described it as "excessive happiness." In another service, all seventy inmates were on their knees because of the power of the Spirit. The anointing of the Spirit often spread revival to many other inmates in the jail. The inmates often conducted their own Bible studies and prayer groups in their housing units. They looked forward all week to my Church services, and they came hungry for the Word and with a desire to seek the Lord. I have chronicled the years of ministry in my two previous books, *In Pursuit of Christ: A Love Story* and *Warrior for Christ: Overcoming Cancer by Faith*. I am so thankful for God's grace to minister to His beloved children for these past twenty-five years. I have a genuine love for all of these precious people, and I continue to pray for them. I look forward to the day that we will be reunited in heaven.

In 1996, the pastor of my Church asked me to take my future wife to the four jail services that we conducted on Friday night. She was a teacher in the women's program, and we became a ministry team for seven years in the jails, prisons, discipleship programs, and nursing homes. We shared the teaching and she sang harmonies with me while I played guitar. My wife was a gifted teacher, singer, and counselor, and we became a great team for the Lord. One of the pastors in the program described our marriage as a "match made in heaven." We were married four years later and we continued to do ministry together for three more years until she decided to stop and find full-time employment. It hasn't always been easy, but by the grace of God, we have remained married for twenty-one years. Recently, I introduced her to Facebook, and she has found a way to minister to many people from all over the world. She is very involved in administering several groups, praying, and supporting people on the Internet. I am thankful to see her using her gifts and ministries to help others.

During this time, the Lord opened doors to do three nursing home services a week. The Holy Spirit did amazing miracles and many were brought to the Lord. The Spirit would raise people out of their wheelchairs, and unresponsive patients would come alive and start singing and laughing. One man was unplugged from his life support machine several days before our weekly service. A woman in a wheelchair informed me of the situation and expressed her belief that "something needed to happen before he passed away." I prayed for him, that angels would take him to heaven, and I then led his two daughters to the Lord. The man died about ten minutes later and the woman in the wheelchair gave her life to Christ in the service. She passed away about two weeks later. The Lord worked for good through this tragedy to bring several people to Christ. By the grace of God, some patients gave their lives to the Lord, but other residents refused to respond to the call of the Holy Spirit. I was wheeling a very thin lady to the service and she looked up to me and said, "I'm dying," I replied, "you need Jesus," but she responded, "no, no, I don't want Jesus, take me back to my room." Sadly, she passed away a couple of weeks later. Jesus had called them for many years to come to Him and be saved, but they refused to listen. I met some amazing believers in these facilities who loved the Lord with all of their hearts. Sadly, I was often their only visitor. Jesus was always with them and angels took them to eternal glory. One precious blind lady played piano for several years in our services. For five years, my wife and I conducted a service for patients with dementia. One man asked us every week for five years whether my wife and I were married. For two years we answered "no," but after we were married we answered "yes" for the next three years. One of the faithful members of our Church passed away during the service, and the residents did not want to be reminded of her death, so we began to say that she was "vacationing in Florida."

It has been a joy to serve under many ministries to the homeless. Unfortunately, most of the programs struggled financially, and several went bankrupt. Ministries to the poor are unable to support themselves and they often need financial assistance from outside sources, such as more affluent Churches. Paul chose to work part-time as a tentmaker to provide for his needs rather than take money from the Churches. For the same reason, I worked part-time as a landscaper for eleven years as I ministered under these faith-based ministries. I distributed flyers on the doors of houses in Phoenix which advertised fifteen dollars to mow the front lawn and an additional ten dollars for the backyard. Gradually, I was hired to do various other jobs such as tree trimming and installing gravel lawns (it's so hot in Phoenix that people often have gravel yards instead of lawns). I lived in a discipleship house for five years and I then moved into an older mobile home north of town. Several years later, the Lord blessed me with a larger mobile home where I continue to live today. The Lord has been faithful to provide for me for the past twenty-five years. The Father has promised to financially provide for all who obey His call into full-time ministry. I have followed the Biblical warning not to get trapped into debt and I have avoided mortgages, new car loans, and credit cards. The book of Proverbs warns, "The rich rules over the poor, and the borrower is the slave of the lender" (Proverbs 22:7). The flesh wants everything now—a big house, new car, new furniture, and expensive clothes, but "Those who desire to be rich fall into temptation, into a snare, into many senseless and hurtful desires that plunge men into ruin and destruction" (1 Timothy 6:9).

The Lord called me to leave the homeless ministry because of widespread sin and immorality. Several months later, the Father opened up a job for me as assistant chaplain at a local homeless mission. I was able to preach short messages to the homeless before every meal and do many Church services in the evening. The head chaplain was very angry and abusive to me and the homeless. They called him "sheriff" and "warden" and no staff at the mission wanted to work for him. He had low blood pressure, and he often raised his heart rate by yelling at a room full of homeless men. He was especially abusive to the disabled who were supposed to go to the front of the food line. He would yell, "I don't believe you are disabled because you can lift more than five pounds." He would intentionally demoralize over a hundred people who were already feeling hopeless, and then tell me that he "felt much better." I complained to the supervisor and he fired me because of a "personality conflict." Some of the staff believed that I was removed because I did the chaplain's job better than the chaplain. A couple of months later, this chaplain tried to fire another staff member, and I wrote a letter to the vice-president describing his abusive behavior. They finally let him go. I was told that he passed away several months later. I am thankful that I was able to minister to many at the mission and lead some of them to Christ. One afternoon, a homeless resident of the mission became very angry because his tools had been stolen. He was yelling with a loud voice at the picnic tables in front of the facility, and I told him that he needed to forgive and let go of the past. He started to shout, "I want God to strike me dead." A short time later, lightning struck the field near where he was standing. The rest of the residents moved away from him because they were afraid that the lightning might kill them also. The Father was merciful that night and he lived for several more years. I continued to minister to him and I assisted his widow after his death.

After serving Christ for eleven and a half years under faith-based ministries, the Lord opened up a full-time job in March of 2006 working as a homeless outreach specialist for a mental health provider. This was my "dream job" where I was paid to outreach homeless, place them into housing, and connect them to services. My boss often told me to "go out and help someone today"—what a job description! I was assigned a company vehicle, and for the next nine and a half years I outreached the homeless at their campsites, on the streets, and in the city parks. I attempted to earn their trust by bringing them food and doing multiple visits. I was able to connect many of them to housing, mental health services, halfway houses, and treatment centers. My office was located in the homeless shelter, and I often did "inreach" to many homeless who were living in the facility. The Lord protected me for nine years while I did outreach alone on Friday nights surrounded by gangs, drug dealers, and people high on drugs and alcohol. I was told by several people that they saw angels protecting me as I walked across the park. The Lord called me to find housing for hundreds of homeless, and I frequently did follow-up visits to teach them life skills such as cooking, cleaning, nutrition, and budgeting. My personal experience with homelessness, poverty, sickness, rejection, and mental illness helped me to have understanding and empathy for those who were suffering on the street. I knew what it felt like to be treated as less than human because I had wandered the streets clothed in rags for seven years as people mocked me or went to the other side of the street to avoid me. The Lord has a purpose for everything that happens in our lives and our suffering is not in vain (2 Corinthians 1:3-4).

9

The Story of Homelessness

"Blessed are the poor in spirit, for theirs is the kingdom
of heaven."

Matthew 5:3

"Blessed is he who considers the poor! The LORD delivers
him in the day of trouble."

Psalms 41:1

"And the master said to the servant, 'Go out to the highways
and hedges, and compel people to come in, that my house may
be filled.'"

Luke 14:23

"The LORD is near the brokenhearted, and saves the crushed
in spirit."

Psalms 34:18

Jesus has called me to minister to hundreds of amazing homeless
people over the past twenty-five years, and many of them became
my close friends. As I write this, my heart is filled with sadness
at the thousands of homeless suffering on the streets in Phoenix and

throughout the world. The Lord gave me His love and compassion for these people in need, and it has been a joy to watch the Lord transform so many lives. In a country with our resources, I believe that we can do much more to assist the poor and the homeless. In my opinion, the government needs to increase funding for housing vouchers and incentives for landowners to build affordable subsidized apartments for low-income individuals. The rental prices in Phoenix have increased substantially and many low-income people are unable to afford an apartment. In addition, many housing complexes currently refuse to work with housing programs for the homeless. There are many causes of homelessness and each situation is unique. In my case, I lost everything due to a serious illness and the lack of help from friends, family, and the government. I believe that increased assistance from friends and family will greatly reduce the number of people living on the street. I suffered in Sun Valley, which is an affluent area with no programs for food distribution and assistance for the poor. I was not eligible for welfare and I had no health insurance for medical treatment. In the book of Acts, the Lord called the Church to provide for those in need, but Christians are not always obedient to Christ (Acts 2:44-45). Some people avoid the street by "couch surfing' at the homes of their friends and family until they are asked to leave. Many live in cars for months or even years, but this is dangerous in Phoenix when the summer temperatures can exceed one hundred and fifteen degrees. Many people struggle to find a safe parking lot, and some lose everything when their vehicle is towed. I have rescued many families from their vehicles and placed them into family shelters where they were often connected to independent housing. I brought many homeless with addiction issues into my home and they often stole my money, debit cards, and even vehicles. I forgave them and the Lord later used me to lead one of them to the Lord. I worked with a twenty-seven-year-old man with mental illness and substance abuse issues who had been rejected by his family. He overdosed on methadone at the shelter and I notified his father by phone. He had been a federal judge on the east coast and he came to Phoenix to film the memorial service. He was amazed as he listened to the testimonies of many people who loved and respected him. He saw his son's value through the eyes of others.

Substance abuse is one of the most obvious causes of homelessness. Unfortunately, once the door is opened to an addiction, it is often difficult to close. I have listened to hundreds of homeless people express a lifetime of regret which resulted from their addiction. Substance abuse has caused many homeless to lose their marriages, children, jobs, and homes. Of course, it is impossible to redo our past life, but I was able to help many people start over. I outreached numerous addicts on the street who looked like skeletons or dead men walking, but they often refused assistance because the drugs had caused them to lose all self-awareness. The enemy was medicating them as he attempted to kill and destroy them. I connected many to residential treatment facilities where they received instruction and counseling. Unfortunately, there are many homeless who are unable to overcome their addiction. I worked with an alcoholic who abandoned his apartment to drink and live on the street in one hundred and five degree temperatures. For many years, he lived on the street and drank until he was admitted into a hospital. When he was released, he returned to the street and the addiction. I have learned that our assistance to people in need will not always be appreciated. I met one alcoholic man who was so intoxicated that he passed out in the middle of a busy street. I rescued him before he was hit by oncoming traffic, and when he woke up, he asked me for a beer—when I declined, he cursed at me. The path of recovery for an addict usually involves many cycles of success and relapse. We are called to love them through the failures, just as Jesus has loved us throughout our lives. I believe that substance abuse is a symptom of deeper issues. People often self-medicate to cover up trauma, broken-ness, bitterness, and unforgiveness that lie deep in their hearts. The Lord can heal the root causes of their addictions and deliver them from this bondage.

In 2006, I was hired as an outreach specialist to focus primarily on the seriously mentally ill who were experiencing homelessness. Several decades ago, mental health providers released many mentally ill out of the mental institutions and connected them to outpatient services. Unfortunately, many of these people disengaged from the services, isolated from society, and self-medicated on street drugs. Without their medication, they often lost self-awareness of their illness. I have witnessed many amazing transformations when the mentally ill were re-connected into treatment. One of my clients with psychosis and schizophrenia spent five years on the street talking to imaginary people. She appeared to have completely lost touch with reality, but she never lost her faith in God. She was very resistant to treatment, so I petitioned her to receive court-ordered mental health services. The Lord performed a miracle and the medication transformed her into a completely different person. She made a video testimony for us, and we were amazed that she had a complete self-awareness of her illness and detailed memory of her years on the street. She seemed to have awakened from a coma with a perfect memory of what had transpired during the time of her unconsciousness. I rejoiced when she returned to her children and regained the life that she had lost. One mentally ill man told me that my voice became one of the voices in his head. I apologized, but he replied, "Your voice is good because it tells me to go to my appointments." I was able to place many seriously mentally ill clients into housing using free homeless vouchers, and I followed up with regular home visits to help them maintain their apartments. Often, the chronically homeless are initially resistant to my efforts to connect them to services. I encountered one lady who was very angry and hostile after five years on the street. I eventually persuaded her to get assistance after I reminded her that she could be reunited with her family. I connected her to housing and mental health services, and she began working as a caregiver for the disabled. She was very artistic and she did a beautiful job decorating her apartment. She has enjoyed many years with her children and grandchildren.

I often felt called by God to assist the most challenging clients. The Lord has given me a patient personality to work with the most difficult cases. I usually gave them my cell phone number and I was frequently dealing with crisis situations on the phone and in person. I spent about ten years working with a homeless man who had severe mental illness and substance abuse issues. Years before, he had suffered a mental breakdown after finding his wife in bed with his best friend. I helped him to obtain an apartment, but he continued to be very angry and obsessed with suicide. I often made calls about his suicidal ideations to his mental health clinic and occasionally to the police. At my suggestion, he went to a nearby Church, but instead of attending the service, he went up to the roof to jump off the building. Thankfully, he decided to come down from the roof and talk to me. We went through a long journey together through many mental hospitals and nursing homes. One day he called me and said, "I'm going to hit them." He was in a mental hospital with one hand on the phone to call me and the other one in a fist threatening to assault several staff members. He was causing a high level of anxiety to the staff at the facility and his doctor said to him, "either you take your medication or I will have to." Unfortunately, a drug dealer "hijacked" his apartment and seriously injured him, and he spent the last two years of his life in a wheelchair at a nursing home. Sadly, he passed away after a hip operation and I posted this memorial for him: "Goodbye my friend, I was proud of the way you turned your life around. We will meet again and walk together in heaven."

I worked with many difficult clients, but one man stands out as the greatest test of my patience. He had serious medical, substance abuse, and mental health issues, and he was transferred to me by another co-worker who refused to work with him. I placed him in multiple apartments, but he was frequently evicted after causing severe damage to the units. He was in his mid-forties, but he often behaved like a young child. He was diagnosed with "explosive personality disorder," which was a nice way of saying that he went into uncontrollable rages. For instance, when the staff at the Social Security office informed him that their records showed that he was deceased, he went into a fit of anger, knocked everything off the tables, and attempted to choke the female staff member. Ironically, he was so upset after Social Security had declared him deceased that he died of a heart attack. Fortunately, the medics were able to revive him. After this episode, he was banned from the office, the sidewalk around the building, and the new office that they moved into several years later. This man was banned from most offices, apartment buildings, banks, and businesses in Phoenix. He "died" again when he was electrocuted while attempting to get his drugs from a high voltage circuit box. Again, the medics were able to revive him. He said later that he thought that it was a safe place to hide his drugs. He passed away for the third time when hospice unplugged him from life support after his internal organs had shut down. We had a "goodbye" party for him with his favorite foods and balloons. He died and his body turned cold and rigid, but the Lord miraculously raised him from the dead. He stayed in hospice for two more weeks and the staff expected him to pass away. He continued to live, and he was transferred into a nursing home and then into independent housing. After this amazing experience, he continued to have his usual bad attitude. When he was frustrated, he would say to me, "it's your fault, this would never have happened if you hadn't raised me from the dead." Of course, I would remind him that Jesus had raised him and not me. I took him to get pizza and he told the staff at the restaurant that "he had been raised from the dead." During this time, he went to see his probation officer in the court building and he set off the alarm at the metal detector. The officers asked him to put his hands up so that they could search him, but he replied, "my pants will fall off." They ordered him again to put up his hands and his pants fell completely down. The next day, I went with him through the same detector and the two officers sang "blue moon" to him. He would test the patience of the staff at the shelter until one worker physically threw him out of the building. The client made a complaint and the staff was fired. I visited him in a padded room in the jail where he had destroyed the padding on one wall with his teeth and fingers. This client attempted multiple escapes from several hospitals. On one occasion, he tried to leave by using an elevator with his IV bag on wheels, but the tube caught in the elevator doors. He was stranded in between floors for several hours until the emergency workers were able to climb down the elevator shaft and rescue him. One day I visited him at the hospital, and he became so upset after I left his room that five security staff rushed past me in the hallway to restrain him. I returned to his room and helped calm him down. I placed him in a nursing home and he almost closed down the facility. He complained to the authorities that there were disabled people on the second story who would not be able to get to safety during a fire. The facility was forced to transfer all of the mobility-impaired residents to the first floor and moved the first-floor patients to the second floor. I could probably write twenty pages of amazing stories about this man—I have never met anyone like him.

Another challenging client was a thirty-four-year-old young man with severe mental illness and brain damage which was caused by his mother's use of drugs during the pregnancy. He was obsessed with the fear of going to hell and became convinced that he needed to castrate himself to go to heaven. He made several attempts (including once on a city bus) and was subsequently placed in several mental hospitals. He then became convinced that he needed to fast for forty days to get into heaven. He was unable to stop eating so he tied himself to a post. When this didn't work, he asked me to take a forty-day vacation to assist him. Instead, I petitioned him to get him court-ordered treatment and he was still tied up when the police came to pick him up. He was transported to a mental health facility where he tried to

Arise, shine; for your light has come, and the glory of the LORD has risen upon you. Isaiah 60:1

escape by jumping into a tree from the second-story window. He was rescued by the EMTs, and his nurse asked him what he learned from the incident. He replied, "I'm not as good of a tree climber as I thought." One day, I found him walking barefoot on the street in one hundred and five degree heat. His feet were burned and we gave him medical attention. He was wearing only underwear and I transported him to obtain clothing. I asked him why he was walking barefoot and he replied, "because Jesus did." I reminded him that Jesus wore sandals and he replied, "I may have to rethink this." He was unable to live independently and he was placed in a mental hospital and then transferred to supervised residential housing. I continued to work with him, and the Lord opened his mind to understand the grace of God and he gave his life to Christ.

I also assisted a sixty-five-year-old Vietnam veteran who was very angry and violent. He was banned from the shelter for assaulting another resident with a two-by-four. He had been an advanced forces army ranger in Vietnam where he was expected to shoot people in the villages and set explosives. He was court martialed for striking a commanding officer when he was startled from behind. Unfortunately, this dishonorable discharge caused him to be exempt from all veteran's services and compensation. He suffered from severe PTSD after the war, but in the seventies, the hospitals did not understand how to effectively treat the illness, so they gave him electric shock therapy. He endured twenty-two years in prison and then spent the remainder of his adult life on the street. He was considered unsuitable for housing by many of the shelter staff. By the grace of God, I was able to obtain housing for him and his life changed dramatically. For several years, he helped me deliver food boxes to my clients. Jesus did a miracle in his life and gave him several visions of heaven. At the shelter, our outreach team worked with a very angry homeless lady in a wheelchair who was frequently yelling and arguing with staff and other residents. Our team was able to place her in housing, but she began fighting with her new neighbors. She was hospitalized with lung cancer and gave her life to Christ at the facility. I held her hand in hospice as Jesus raised her to be with Him forever. I spoke at her memorial service at the shelter, and I testified of her conversion and resurrection into heaven.

I worked with several extremely intelligent clients, including a client who had been a Harvard graduate and a professor at Brown University. She lost her job and became homeless after developing schizophrenia. She had forgotten about her Social Security checks and she had accumulated over twelve thousand dollars of back pay. I helped her obtain the money in cash from a check-cashing business because she had no identification card to obtain a bank account. She wanted to stay at the shelter with the money, but I advised against it for safety reasons. She decided to go to the airport and fly to another city. I worked with another homeless client who had been one of the top attorneys in the country until he developed schizophrenia. He spent several hundred thousand dollars traveling to Washington D.C. and other governmental offices in an attempt to convince them that there was a conspiracy to take away his employment. One of my homeless clients lived in the yard of a woman whose house of so full of her possessions that she had to live in her car. She also "hoarded" multiple homeless people that she picked up on the street. She collected seven large dogs and about twenty cats who lived in the backyard, which was also filled with her possessions. The City of Phoenix had removed her from several previous houses and they were in the process of evicting her again. Fortunately, I was able to rescue him from this situation and place him in his own apartment. I met many homeless people with schizophrenia that traveled from state to state for many years on the bus or plane to escape from imaginary conspiracies. I worked with many clients with remarkable delusions that they were God, Jesus, the king of England, famous movie stars, a U.S. president, or the owner of the shelter facility. I received some amazing calls from mentally ill clients, including one client who warned me not to eat potato chips because they are "hyper-accessing us through potato chips."

Sadly, there are many homeless with chronic medical conditions. Some were discharged from hospitals and nursing homes to the shelter when their health insurance no longer paid for their treatment. Many clients were misinformed by the hospital staff that a medical bed was waiting for them at the shelter. They were frequently released on Friday night because there was less staff to stop the discharge. One man was dropped-off multiple times at the shelter in a wheelchair, and we often found him on Monday morning covered with feces and hundreds of flies. I located the hospital that was repeatedly releasing him to the shelter, and I warned the supervisor that I would notify the newspapers if they wrongfully discharged him again. I also traced some of the other improper releases to several nursing homes and I advised them to find a more appropriate method of discharging their patients. One doctor from the shelter clinic was so upset with the treatment of these clients that she started a nursing facility for the homeless. I have taken many homeless with serious health issues to the ER, including one man with gangrene and maggots. The nurses didn't want to touch him, so they asked us to take off his pants before he was treated. Ironically, the nurse informed us that the maggots probably kept him alive by eating the infected flesh. Our outreach team would often petition clients who refused medical treatment for their severe medical issues. I teamed up with a co-worker to provide housing for a homeless woman with terminal cancer who had been released from a nursing home to live on the street in temperatures that were over one hundred degrees. I also placed a woman into housing with her teenage daughter. Sadly, one year later, she developed terminal cancer and her doctors were unable to stop the spread of the disease with chemotherapy. She arranged to have hospice come to her home so she could be with her daughter. I visited her regularly, brought her monthly food boxes, and obtained rental assistance from our company. I tried to encourage her through this difficult journey, and I was heartbroken as I watched the twenty tumors gradually take her life away until she died one year later. The goal for many homeless people is usually to find housing, but after they move off the street, they must face other difficult issues in their lives. One man in a wheelchair was very excited to obtain housing, but he hung himself several months later because his ex-wife would not let him see his daughter. Another client attempted suicide by taking about seventy prescription pills. I visited her in the hospital where she confessed that she had obeyed the voice of the devil when she took the medication. By the grace of God, she survived. Several of my chronically homeless clients have passed away in their apartments from health issues caused by decades of substance abuse and homelessness. The shelter was located in a dangerous area called the "zone," and one of my clients was murdered with a knife after a disagreement with another man in the lunch line. Sometimes people can be disappointing. One Friday night while I was doing outreach in one of the parks, I met a group of homeless men sitting on a picnic table and getting high on drugs. I noticed a man laying on the grass near the table and I asked them what had happened to him. They replied about four hours earlier he had said something about his head and then fell backward onto the ground. The rest of the group continued to do drugs and they never checked on their friend. I went over to him and determined that he was dead. I called the police and immediately the men packed up and left the area. They were "unable" to check on their friend's welfare, but they could move quickly when they heard the police were coming. I convinced one of them to stay to make a police report, and he admitted that their behavior was "pretty bad."

Some chronically homeless become "addicted" to the freedom— no jobs, bills, or responsibilities. I have offered assistance to many homeless who declined all services. For instance, I met one fifty-seven-year-old homeless man in the park and offered to help him find a job and an apartment. He told me that he had never worked or lived in his own home in his entire adult life. I asked him why and he replied, "I argued with my parents when I was eighteen." I waited for further explanation, but that was his whole story. He used the fight with his parents as an excuse for thirty-nine years of homelessness. I repeated my offer to help him find a job and an apartment and he replied, "I've made it this far, I will just coast the rest of the way." In his mind, he blamed his parents, but it had been his choice to be homeless. I have housed several clients into nice apartments, who later chose to walk away and return to the street. I moved one elderly man in a wheelchair into a brand-new apartment in a senior living complex, but he moved back to the street one month later because he "didn't want to be around old people."

Lack of money is a major reason for homelessness, and the rental prices are so high in Phoenix that many people with Social Security and minimum wage jobs can not afford to rent apartments. I helped many homeless obtain housing through free housing vouchers, but there were long waiting lists for these programs. I collaborated with several landlords to lower the initial costs required to move into a unit. About twelve years ago, there was a high vacancy rate in Phoenix and I made arrangements for apartment owners and managers to come down to the shelter with their laptops and sign people up for housing. They were willing to lower the move-in costs to only seventy-nine dollars, and by the grace of God, I was able to house seventy-eight homeless in one apartment complex. It was a win-win situation: the owners filled up their buildings with renters, and many homeless were able to obtain housing. I found an apartment for one man who had been homeless for twenty-five years. His name was "soda pop" because he earned money selling cold drinks out of his ice chest with wheels. For the first two weeks, he slept outside his apartment on the pavement, but he adjusted to living indoors and stayed there for many years. Over the last several years, it has become much more difficult for the homeless to obtain housing because of increased rental prices. Many apartment complexes now require the prospective tenant to earn two to three times the rental amount. After the clients were housed, I did follow-up visits and connected them with medical, mental health, and substance abuse services. I also helped many obtain disability benefits and employment. Some of my clients became homeless after losing their fortunes. For example, one shelter resident had lost five hundred thousand dollars in penny stocks when the market collapsed in 2008. He complained to me that there was no room service at the facility. Another man showed up in my office with a wig, dress, and high heels after losing one million dollars in the real estate collapse. Everyone deals with trauma differently. I assisted many families living on the street after being evicted from their apartments. The family shelter was frequently full, and the only way to find a bed for them was to transport them in a police vehicle.

Criminal history is also a major barrier for the homeless, and many employers and apartment owners will not accept felons. I developed relationships with landlords who were willing to give them a second chance. I referred clients to an employment service located at our shelter that specialized in finding jobs for felons. Many homeless had lost hope of obtaining housing and they were filled with joy when they moved into their new apartment. Some of them became "institutionalized" after many years in prison. One man was so afraid of living on the outside that he tried to turn himself into the local jail. They would not accept him, so he stole a car from a dealership and drove for about forty miles to the gate of a prison, where they arrested him. I saw the Lord do many miracles in courtrooms on behalf of members of our discipleship program. In one case, the judge had already announced in the courtroom that he was sentencing my client to two and a half years in prison. I spoke on his behalf and asked the court to release him so he could finish our discipleship program. The judge asked the prosecutor whether he had any objections, and the Lord wouldn't let the prosecutor speak (he appeared to be choking). The judge ruled, "because the prosecutor has no objections, I release the defendant to finish the program." In another case, the judge had already announced his decision to sentence a member of our ministry to two and a half years in prison. However, this was not the plan of God, and for several minutes, the judge fought the will of the Lord. The judge kept repeating, "I don't want to do this" and "I don't know why I'm doing this" until he decided to release him. I have also seen God intervene to release an innocent man charged with murder. We first met in the hallway of the jail, and he described with tears how he had spent the previous year in jail for a murder that he didn't commit. Fortunately, his wife stood by him and supported him through this whole ordeal. The man who had committed the murder was already in prison for the crime. The detective had coerced a witness to testify against this man by threatening him with prison. The defense attorney played a tape recording that provided proof of the detective's intimidation of the witness. On the tape, the witness had originally stated that he knew nothing about the murder and the detective threatened him several times by asking, "do you want to go back to jail?" Under duress, the witness changed his testimony and stated that the defendant had committed the murder. The witness had been addicted to drugs at the time of the murder, and the defense attorney put up a picture of him with long hair and dirty clothes. The prosecutor had cleaned up the witness for the trial and kept "accidentally" knocking over the unfavorable photo of the witness. There was much joy when the defendant was found "not guilty" and his wife arranged for a limo and the news stations to be waiting for him outside the jail. We remained friends for years and I helped him heal from the bitterness that resulted from the ordeal.

I was able to rescue many prostitutes from the street. For example, I worked with a twenty-two-year-old woman who had already given birth to seven babies from prostitution. Child Protection Services had placed all of the babies into foster care or adoption. Her eighth child was born prematurely, addicted to drugs, and weighed only one pound and six ounces. Amazingly, the hospital kept it alive, and they found a couple from Belgium to adopt the child. Shortly after the adoption, she decided to move to another state and started a new way of life. I was also able to rescue many women from abusive relationships and place them into safe domestic violence shelters. For example, I transported one injured woman to the shelter and then to the hospital. Unfortunately, despite my warnings, she returned to her abusive partner. On one occasion, the abuser tried to break through a locked door at the shelter to attack my client. Many women revealed to me that they had been sexually abused as children and then entered into abusive relationships as an adult. I worked for many years with a client who was seriously mentally ill, a drug dealer, and a heroin addict with anorexia. She only weighed ninety pounds when I first met her and I connected her to several appropriate treatment programs. I obtained an apartment for her through a free housing voucher for the mentally ill, and she has continued to live in her home for over ten years (which was longer than any other person in the program). She overcame her anorexia, maintained her sobriety, and she has been married for over eight years.

During this time, the city of Phoenix passed a law making it illegal to feed the homeless, and the police prevented all individuals and Churches from distributing food to the poor. The authorities believed that the food was attracting the homeless to downtown Phoenix. One day, I was chased by a police car after handing out lunches while outreaching the homeless. For about fifteen minutes, the officer expressed his anger about all the "terrible things" that the homeless were doing to the city. Fortunately, I was not arrested, and I discreetly continued to do outreach to the homeless and distribute lunches. I was disappointed that in Phoenix it was now illegal to obey the command of Jesus to feed the poor. It was also illegal to camp in Phoenix, and the police often awakened the homeless at night, gave them tickets, and ordered them to leave the area. Several years ago, the U.S. Supreme Court overturned these laws and there are now many homeless openly camping in Phoenix and across the country.

Sadly, many homeless die every year in the summer heat in Phoenix where the temperatures can reach as high as one hundred and seventeen degrees Fahrenheit. Regrettably, some homeless pass out on the street and are "cooked' on the pavement. Our outreach team spent many hours in the summer distributing thousands of bottles of water to the homeless and helped them to find emergency shelters. Some of the homeless were so mentally ill that they wore thick ski jackets in the excessive heat. For many years, the city of Phoenix opened emergency overflow shelters in the summer to prevent heat-related deaths. Every spring, the city threatened to close the overflow shelter due to a lack of funding. In response, our outreach team organized several homeless marches from the shelter to the state capitol to advocate for shelter funding. The shelters remained open for several years, but they were eventually closed. In response, the shelter then opened up their day room to permit the homeless to sleep inside at night. After several years, the overflow shelters were completely closed, but several Churches permitted the homeless to stay in their air-conditioned facilities during the daytime. Some of the homeless were amazing self-advocates. One of my clients had lost his electric wheelchair when the EMTs transported him to the hospital. He received no response from the EMTs, so he made a protest sign and sat in his non-motorized wheelchair in front of city hall until they replaced his equipment. The city of Phoenix decided to buy him a new, seven thousand dollar electric wheelchair rather than risk the bad publicity.

I often ministered in dangerous areas, and the Lord has always protected me from harm. One day after visiting a nursing home, I was robbed in my car by a man high on crack who was working for a nearby drug house. He held a gun to my head for about ten minutes while worship music played on my stereo. God was in control and I made arrangements for him to take the $180 and return my wallet. I told him I wouldn't chase him as he left on his bike. I saw a policeman sitting in his car a couple of blocks away and I informed him that I had just been robbed at gunpoint. He replied that I should call 911—he was busy sitting in his car. One day, I was witnessing in the "zone" and saw five men in a circle selling drugs, so I put a tract on top of the cocaine that said "Jesus Loves You" in bold letters. God's angels were protecting me for many years as I did outreach among drug dealers and gang members. At one homeless program, I encountered a psychotic veteran from Desert Storm who believed that he was still in the war. He began threatening to kill about twenty people who were eating dinner at the facility. The Lord guided me to have the security officer pose as his commanding officer and he told the veteran to "stand down."

Doing outreach to the homeless is like mining for diamonds—many appear rough on the outside, but with God's love and grace, they become the precious people that God created them to be. I shared God's love with many who had lost their hope after years of failures and rejection. Many homeless will respond when they see that someone truly cares for them. Jesus called me to give hope to those who had lost hope and believe in people who no longer believed in themselves. I saw them through the eyes of Christ and told them the good news of the Gospel that God loves them and there is forgiveness of sins through Jesus. I met hundreds of beautiful believers with kind and generous hearts who were living on the street. Please pray for them—many had been forgotten by the world, but in God's eyes, they are very precious.

Your divine throne endures for ever and ever. Your royal scepter is a scepter of equity. Psalms 4506

10

Season of Suffering

"Count it all joy, my brethren, when you meet various
trials, for you know that the testing of your faith produces
steadfastness And let steadfastness have its full effect, that
you may be perfect and complete, lacking in nothing."

James 1:2-4

"Be sober, be watchful. Your adversary the devil prowls
around like a roaring lion, seeking someone to devour. Resist
him, firm in your faith, knowing that the same experience
of suffering is required of your brotherhood throughout
the world."

1 Peter 5:8-9

The Father blessed me for about two decades with good health, a great ministry, and trips to the mountains, but my life changed dramatically in 2015 when the Lord called me into my second season of suffering. I prayed for many years to know Christ regardless of the cost, and I would not trade my friendship with Christ for all the treasures of the world. I refused to compromise and I was willing to suffer the loss of all things to gain Christ (Philippians 3:7-8). The early Church was also called to walk the way of the Cross and suffer for Christ (Mark 10:28-30). The intense spiritual warfare began when my family located me through an attorney working for my mother's estate. The enemy began by inflicting me with stage four incurable Non-Hodgkin's Lymphoma. My initial symptoms were respiratory issues, anemia, and fatigue. Gradually, the cancer in my bone marrow began to cause deterioration of my bones and severe pain in my hips and back. I could no longer hike, bike ride, or take vacations to the mountains. The enemy also moved to take away my wonderful job as an outreach specialist when the grant for our program was given to another local provider. It seemed like a dream, as we packed up twenty years of paperwork and equipment and sold the vehicles. Fortunately, the Lord provided another job with the same company assisting mentally ill individuals to obtain and maintain housing. At first, the job was a blessing, but the enemy gradually increased the workload to about three times the amount that was originally required. The employer expected me to complete a service plan, a mental health assessment, and about eighteen other documents for each client. Our supervisors continually monitored our location with tracking apps on our phones. One of my co-workers stopped to get gas and use the facilities, and immediately received a call from her supervisor asking why she had spent twenty minutes at the station. I did not enjoy this micro-management after experiencing the freedom of my previous job. In addition, my employer required me to write daily progress notes so that the company could bill Medicaid. The management began to record how much money we were bringing in every month, and the supervisors gradually increased the required amount to ten thousand dollars per month. My health began to deteriorate as I was forced to work an extra two hours a day without pay to bring in the required amount of money. Many co-workers were fired or quit under this pressure. By the grace of God, I was given an award in 2018 for "Employee of the Year" while working with stage four cancer. I was blessed to help so many homeless people find and maintain housing, but the job was becoming increasingly stressful. The supervisors turned many of my co-workers against me by telling them, "If Peter can make ten thousand dollars a month with cancer, then so can you." One of the supervisors reported at a staff meeting that they were "working Peter to death." I complained to my supervisor and the director about the unreasonable workload, but the director accused me of being "insubordinate." My supervisor said that they would "not make allowances for my stage four cancer" and she frequently pressured me to retire. Fortunately, my intermittent FMLA required them to give me periodic days off for my illness. The situation became too stressful, and I moved to another job in the same company where I assisted inmates in successfully transitioning from jail into treatment services and halfway houses.

Unfortunately, my health continued to decline in the next six months and I was forced to take sick leave several times due to the cancer, pneumonia, and an inner ear issue that caused vertigo. I occasionally experienced persecution from fellow workers during my employment. For example, one of my co-workers came very close to me in a threatening manner and started mocking me that I had been seriously ill for three weeks with pneumonia (note: this illness can be fatal for those who have Non-Hodgkin's Lymphoma). In July of 2018, I suffered a compression fracture of my spine when I attempted to get out of bed on a Sunday morning. I drove to my primary care doctor with a broken back, but they failed to see the fracture when they viewed the X-ray. My pain grew worse, and the next day my wife drove me to my cancer clinic where they determined that I had a compression fracture of my L5 vertebrae. The surgeon performed a kyphoplasty surgery to repair my spine, and the pathologist determined that the cancer was in ninety percent of my bone marrow. My supervisor was threatening to fire me, so I returned to work ten days before my back was completely healed. My surgeon authorized me to return to work because he did not understand the severity of the damage to my back. By the end of the first week, the pain became too severe to continue and the company dismissed me after thirteen and a half years of employment. I believe that the job pressure to return to work prematurely resulted in additional fractures to my spine. I spent the next five months confined in a chair with intense back pain as the cancer caused ten more compression fractures to my vertebrae. The pain was so severe that I needed to lift myself up by my arms twenty-four hours a day for five months to lessen the pressure on my back. I endured this suffering by crying out to Jesus for mercy and grace as He carried me through this very difficult time. The Lord raised me up to walk with a walker and minister in the jails for two months until they were closed for COVID twenty-two months ago. I now minister to many on Facebook where I post Bible study videos, pray and support many people who are suffering from cancer and other illnesses. I have provided over thirty Bible study videos for the inmates in the jail which they can access through their tablets. The Lord has opened doors to preach at multiple crusades in Pakistan, and by the grace of God, many have been saved, delivered, and healed. Thank you, Jesus! The Father has begun to fulfill His vision that I would preach the Gospel to many nations. The Father has promised to heal my cancer and my back fractures so that I can preach to the world. The complete story of my cancer journey is described in my book, *Warrior for Christ: Overcoming Cancer by Faith.*

11

The Will of God

"Therefore do not be foolish, but understand what the will of the Lord is."

Ephesians 5:17

"If you love me, you will keep my commandments."

John 14:15

"For I have come down from heaven, not to do my own will, but the will of him who sent me."

John 6:38

The will of God is holy and sacred, and I choose to bow down to Him and obey His plan for my life. When God calls, I reply, "Yes Lord, I will do all that You have commanded." I have learned that "God is God and I am not," and that I do not have the right to question His Word or His will. Faith is obeying God unconditionally, without questioning His plan. I may not always understand God's ways, but I trust that Jesus will always lead me closer to the Father (John 14:6). By faith, Abraham obeyed God's call to leave his homeland, and he went out not knowing where he was going (Hebrews 11:8-9). I exist to worship and serve my Creator.

Jesus died on the Cross for my sins and I would never ask Him, "what more can you do for me?" I have learned that God's ways are not my ways and His will is not my will. The Lord teaches in Isaiah, "For my thoughts are not your thoughts, neither are your ways my ways, says the LORD. For as the heavens are higher than the earth, so are my ways higher than your ways and my thoughts than your thoughts" (Isaiah 55:8-9). The Lord is asking us to trust Him and obey His purpose and plan for our lives which He created in Christ before we were born (Ephesians 2:10). Jesus is the only constant in my life, and I must be ready to follow Him whenever He calls me. We are in this world but not of it, and like Abraham, we are just "pitching our tents" in this life. Our sinful nature will choose the wide path with no suffering, but Jesus calls us to deny ourself, take up our cross and follow Him on the narrow path of life (Matthew 16:24). The plan of God will always be a mystery to us in this life. I love the adventure of seeking the God who created the universe with one word. He has called us to live by faith and trust Him without having all the answers. Some Christians try to bring God down to a level that they can intellectually understand—how boring! I want to take Jesus out of the "religious box" and proclaim that He is the awesome eternal Creator who is greater than anything we can imagine. The Lord has given to us His Word with all the information we need to believe in Him and be saved. "The secret things belong to the LORD our God; but the things that are revealed belong to us and to our children for ever, that we may do all the words of this law" (Deuteronomy 29:29). If it is not in the Bible, then we don't need to know it. John writes, "Now Jesus did many other signs in the presence of the disciples, which are not written in this book; but these are written that you may believe that Jesus is the Christ, the son of God, and that believing you may have life in His name." (John 20:30-31).

One of the most popular false gospels today is called the "word-faith movement" or the "name it and claim it gospel." In this false teaching, many are told that those who have faith can command God to obey their will. They believe that their faith has enough power to compel God to give them healing, success, and money. They mis-interpret this scripture: "Therefore I tell you, whatever you ask in prayer, believe that you have received it, and it will be yours" (Mark 11:24). John writes that God will only answer prayers that are made according to His will (1 John 5:14-15). I have spent many years studying the Bible and seeking the whole truth that God has revealed to us through His Word. I often do complete word studies on prayer and other subjects, rather than making a doctrine out of one scrip-ture. Some adherents of this heresy believe that sickness and poverty are a result of unbelief. In one Church, I was thrown out and labeled a Satanist because I had been sick. Another pastor pointed me out in Church and said, "Anyone who says that we have to suffer is of the devil." This false teaching comes from the original sin of pride that exalts man to "become like God knowing good and evil" (Genesis 3:5). It is time to humble ourselves before God, because the fear of the Lord is the beginning of wisdom. The Scriptures instruct us to "offer to God acceptable worship, with reverence and awe, for our God is a consuming fire" (Hebrews 12:28). I have learned to have respect and reverence for the Lord and His will. Those who follow this false teaching seek to make Jesus into a "Santa Claus" who exists for our pleasure. Several years ago, I attended a Church where the pastor told us to make a list of fifteen things that we desired and the

Lord would automatically give them to us. I stood up and declared that this was not the true gospel, and I was eventually thrown out of the Church. I listened to a famous preacher teach that God was going to give everyone in the Church five new mansions and five new Mercedes Benz cars. This lie was extremely popular, and security was called to calm down the listeners. The Spirit revealed to me that they were worshiping the golden calf. The book of James warns that God will not answer prayers for the gratification of our fleshly desires. Those who love the world do not love the Lord (1 John 2:15-17). It is the enemy that offers us the things of this world in exchange for our souls (Luke 4: 5-8). The Lord will not answer prayers that are contrary to His will. For example, God did not remove Paul's thorn in the flesh because He was using the suffering to keep Paul humble so that His power could work through him (2 Corinthians 12:7-11). Moses prayed to go into the promised land, but it was the Lord's will for him to die on a mountain on the other side of the Jordan river (Deuteronomy 4:6-10). Jesus taught us to pray for strength to surrender to His authority and obey His will: "Your kingdom come, your will be done, on earth as it is in heaven" (Matthew 6:10).

I have learned over the past forty-six years that there is a big difference between my will, which is influenced by the flesh, and the will of the eternal, holy, and righteous God. Jesus has led me through many glorious mountain top experiences, but He has also called me to valleys of intense suffering. My flesh would never choose the way of the Cross, yet I have often prayed in the Spirit to know Christ at any cost. The Spirit put a passion in my heart for Jesus to refine me and remove anything in me that is not of Him. The Lord chose my path and I decided to obey Him. My flesh would have preferred to be born into a comfortable and loving family, but instead, I was raised in a hostile and hateful environment. God works in all things for good, and this childhood trauma led me to seek Him with all of my heart. The Lord delivered me from darkness and oppression and healed my hardened heart. Jesus revealed Himself to me in the seventies when I was born again and baptized in the Holy Spirit. For three and a half years, I walked in the Spirit as I enjoyed the fellowship of a loving, Spirit-filled Church. During this time, the Lord appeared to me in glory with angels surrounding me and He called me into a special relationship with Him. I envisioned a glorious future walking with God, but I was surprised when the Lord revealed to me that I was called to suffer for Christ. I wanted to stay in this wonderful fellowship of believers, but God's plan was to lead me into the wilderness where He would discipline and refine me so that I would become more like Christ. Jesus called me to lay down my life in this world and leave behind this Church, my homeland, and the family that had disowned me. The Holy Spirit led my wife and me to move to the mountains of Idaho where I intended to start a landscaping business and enjoy God's beautiful creation. Instead, God's will for me was for me to endure the refining fire of a seven-year illness. The Lord told me that I would not be content with my life in Idaho, but that I would be content with Him.

The Father gave me the power to lay down my life and He promised to raise me up with Christ (John 10:18). Our greatest expression of love for Christ is to lay down our lives for Him, believing that the Lord will raise us by His power. Jesus asked me if I loved Him more than my healthy body, and I worshiped God by offering my body as a living sacrifice to Him (Romans 12:1; John 21:15-19). The illness destroyed my body and swelled it out beyond recognition. I had climbed many mountains, but for seven years I would only be able to walk a couple of feet at a time. The Lord also asked me to lay down my mental abilities, my two college degrees, and everything that I had learned in nineteen years of school. In my love for Jesus, I gave it all back to God, and the sickness erased my memory and I no longer remembered that two-plus-two equals four. The Father created me and He asked me whether I loved Him more than my life in this world, and I surrendered my life to Him. The poisons in my body erased all memory of who I was and of my life in this world. I no longer remembered that I used to ski or hike in the mountains. The Lord had blessed me with good mental health and He asked me to lay this down before Him. The poisons in my body caused me to become seriously mentally ill with severe depression, schizophrenia, OCD, and extreme anger. I laid down my family, friends, and the joy of fellowship that I had experienced in the Charismatic Church. I now faced seven years of isolation and suffering with no support or assistance. I was called to face this suffering alone, but Jesus is always with me. Christ also suffered alone on the Cross after his disciples turned away from`Him. Most of Paul's friends abandoned him at the end of his life as he faced execution (2 Timothy 1:15; 4:9-11). By the grace of God, I was able to walk with Him through this illness that took away my body and all memory, because with God all things are possible. According to His promise, He healed me and restored my life. I am living proof that the Lord still does miracles today! I was crucified with Christ and now He lives in me forevermore. The Father led me into a season of healing and restoration from the trauma of the illness. The Lord raised me up with the resurrection power of Christ and healed my body, restoring my memory and my mental health. My Creator knew me, and He re-created me in the image of Christ. To use computer language, my files were deleted, but the Lord kept a backup file and He downloaded it into me. We serve a truly amazing God. The Father restored my life and blessed my landscaping business as I walked with Him for seven years in the mountains of Idaho. These were some of the most enjoyable years of my life as I skied, hiked, cross-country skied, and rode my motorcycle and bicycle. I saved up money for seven years and I planned to buy an inexpensive house in a nearby town. I loved Idaho and intended to live the rest of my life in Sun Valley.

Once again, the Lord had a different plan, and He called me to leave my life in the mountains and move to Phoenix to minister to the homeless and those in nursing homes and jails for the next twenty-five years. I was called out of my comfort zone in Sun Valley to live and minister to people in need in the inner-city of Phoenix. I had planned to continue this ministry for many more years, but God's will was to call me to suffer again for Christ. I was diagnosed with stage four Non-Hodgkin's Lymphoma, which caused eleven compression fractures of my vertebrae. The illness caused me to lose my job working with the homeless and in the past thirty months, my faith has been tested with severe pain and isolation. I have learned to proclaim as Jesus did in the Garden of Gethsemane, "Not my will, but Thy will be done" (Matthew 26:39). I live by faith as I glorify Him through this illness and wait for His promised healing. I cried out to the Lord, and He has raised me up to walk by faith. I had never been on Facebook, but almost two years ago, the Lord opened doors to minister to thousands through the Internet.

The Father has taught me to rely on Him and pray before making any important decision. The scriptures teach us to "Trust in the LORD will all your heart, and do not rely on your own insight. In all your ways acknowledge him, and he will make straight your paths. (Proverbs 3:5-6). The Father has created a specific plan for each of our lives and we choose whether we will obey His will. For instance, Jeremiah was called to be a prophet before he was created (Jeremiah 1:5), and Paul was set apart to preach the Gospel before he was born (Galatians 1:15-16). Unfortunately, some rely on their own understanding, which often results in much needless suffering. Years ago, I advised one of the men in our discipleship program to pray before he married a woman in the discipleship program, but he replied that the Church was already rented and he didn't have the time to pray. As a result, his marriage was a disaster—he left his wife on the wedding night and spent the next five years in prison. After his release, he forced his wife to work as a prostitute to support their drug addiction. He chose to follow his own path which led to destruction (Proverbs 16:25). In the same Church, there was a man who was in charge of the prayer ministry who had prayed for a wife for five years. It seemed that his request had been answered when a beautiful woman came to our Church who appeared to be very spiritual. The prayer minister leaned to his own understanding and married her after two weeks without consulting the Lord. She was a Satanist sent by the devil to trap a believer into marriage. She drove him out of his own home in two weeks and he fell away from God and left the Church. The devil disguises himself as an angel of light and his servants as servants of righteousness (2 Corinthians 11:14-15).

The Lord loves us and cares about our everyday lives, and He wants us to pray and seek His will in every important decision that we make. The Lord blesses our lives when we obey Him, but our ways lead us into needless suffering. For example, several years ago, I bought an older sports car without consulting the Lord. The sellers were thieves who turned back the odometer reading and the car was a disaster that completely died on a busy freeway. I began praying for another vehicle, and during this time, I went on a missionary trip to Mexico and rode with the pastor in a rental Nissan Altima. I liked the car and continued to pray for the Father to provide a vehicle. The Lord began to show me many Altimas on the road in various colors, and He asked me which color I liked best. I chose the red one, and the Spirit led me to search for Altimas on the internet, but they were all too expensive. Finally, the Lord told me to type the exact amount that I could afford, and the picture of the car showed on the screen. It was a salvaged vehicle that was selling for several thousand dollars less than the other cars advertised on the internet. I decided to buy the car. I borrowed money from my retirement account, but the first check was lost in the mail. The enemy was resisting God's plan and the owner was getting impatient. Thankfully, the check finally arrived and I purchased the car, which has been the best one that I have ever owned. Life is so much better when we let God direct our steps. Thank you, Jesus.

12

Sorrow

"In this world you will have tribulation, but be of good cheer,
I have overcome the world."

John 16:33

"He was despised and rejected by men; a man of sorrows, and
acquainted with grief."

Isaiah 53:3

"May those who sow in tears reap with shouts of joy!"

Psalms 126:5

The Lord has blessed me with tremendous joy as I have walked with Him in heavenly places, but I have also experienced great sorrow from many years of suffering and rejection. As I have explained in the previous chapters, I have endured much suffering from two terminal illnesses and considerable sorrow from the rejection of my mother, family, wife, best friends, classmates, and fellow Christians. I diligently prayed for all of these people, but they chose to walk in the ways of the enemy—hate, unforgiveness, and jealousy. Looking back on my life, I realize that my relationship with the Lord has replaced the lack of love from my family, friends, and the Church. The persecution and hate that I have experienced in this life have caused me to seek God with all my heart. The Lord is everything in my life—His love is all I need. I have walked with the Father as a friend for over forty-seven years and I rely on Him to carry me through all of the tribulations and persecution of this world. The wickedness on this earth has caused most men's love to grow cold (Matthew 24:12). Jesus was despised and rejected, a man of sorrows and acquainted with grief (Isaiah 53:3). The Lord's sorrow in the Garden of Gethsemane was so severe that it was almost to the point of death. Paul wrote that he was so utterly and unbearably crushed by his suffering that he despaired of life itself (2 Corinthians 1:8-9). I have often felt overwhelmed by the sorrow, but I have learned to pray and pour out my heart to Jesus. I walk by faith above the suffering, just as Peter did when he walked on water (Matthew 14:23-33). When my faith weakens, I sometimes "sink" into depression and despair. I have learned to cry out to Jesus, and He lifts me up to walk with Him in heavenly places. One of the most difficult moments in my life occurred when I was near death from starvation and a terminal illness, and my family refused to give me even the scraps from their table. I knocked on the door of their expensive vacation home, clothed in rags in below zero temperatures, and they refused to acknowledge that I had been a part of the family. My heart was also broken when my wife lost her faith during the seven-year illness and turned away from God to join the devil. She left me and began practicing witchcraft against me. The enemy has tempted most of my best friends to betray me, and I have been rejected by multiple Churches and ministries. I have learned to put my trust in God, and His love has never failed me. Many years ago, the Father told me to pray that He would send me to a place where there is no rejection for me—I am still praying. Over two years ago, I experienced another time of sorrow when I was confined to a chair and unable to move for five months from eleven compression fractures of my vertebrae caused by stage four cancer. After spending the past twenty-five years helping people in need, I could not find anyone to assist me for a couple of hours a day. Only one friend offered to help me, but then demanded one thousand dollars a month (which was ninety percent of my income). Jesus commanded us to visit the sick and help those in need, but only four friends visited me during these two years of suffering. (Matthew 25:31-46). Most of my friends disappeared when I became sick; others said that they were too busy to talk and some told me that it was too depressing to hear about my suffering. I thought that if it is depressing to hear about my pain, then imagine what it would be like to live through it. The Lord gave me a vision of my situation—I was standing in a field talking about my suffering, and about one hundred people were walking around in circles. The Spirit revealed to me that my friends were too busy with their jobs, families, and socializing to listen or to help me. Jesus was always with me and He heard all of my cries for mercy and grace. Jesus raised me up and I am walking again. Thankfully, He has opened doors for support from people all over the world on Facebook. I was recently asked in an interview about my cancer journey, "What did you learn from your experience with cancer?" I replied, "To rely on Jesus—I need Him every second of every day." My health, friends, work, and ministry were gone, but Jesus is all I needed. I have forgiven them and Jesus has healed my heart. I have learned to spend several hours a day praying and giving my burdens to Jesus, and I honestly believe that without His healing, the sorrow of my life would have crushed me. I am now free from the past to follow Christ and help those in need for the rest of my life. I have learned to forget what lies behind and press on to the upward call of God in Christ (Philippians 3:13-14).

Some may ask, "why did your wife, family, friends, and Churches betray and reject you?" The Bible teaches that our enemies will be from our own household and that we will be persecuted and hated by all nations (Matthew 10:34-37; 24:9). I have been amazed at how easily the enemy can "whisper lies" into the ear of a loved one and deceive them to become critical, judgmental, jealous, or angry. Satan cannot control those who truly walk in the Spirit, but he can easily influence anyone who is lukewarm and walk in the ways of sin. The devil will target the strongest followers of Christ because he considers them a threat to his kingdom of darkness. For example, when Paul went into a town preaching the Gospel or doing miracles, the enemy inspired strong persecution against him. Those who walk in the devil's ways of anger, jealousy, pride, hate, and condemnation are easily manipulated by the enemy. The religious leaders of Christ's time pretended to know God, but they actually worshiped and obeyed the devil. Jesus told them, "You are of your father the devil, your will is to do your father's desires" (John 8:44). The devil disguises himself as an angel of light and his followers are disguised as servants of righteousness (2 Corinthians 11:14-15). These leaders chose to yield their will to obey Satan's plan to crucify Jesus. Jesus is God and He came to this earth and healed the sick, raised the dead, and delivered many from demons, but Satan blinded them so they did not recognize Him or believe the signs that He performed. They accused the holy and righteous God of sin because He broke their Sabbath rules. In the same way, the devil was able to turn my loved ones against me with his lies and deception. He tempted them to be jealous and judge me without cause. Satan is called the accuser, and he often uses the mouths of those close to us to attack us. Even Peter was deceived by the enemy to attack Jesus because he didn't understand the message of the Cross. Jesus rebuked Satan when he heard his voice speaking through Peter. In the same way, I have often heard the voice of Satan speaking through those closest to me. They were deceived to think that Satan's voice of condemnation was the righteous judgment of God. The Bible warns us to test every spirit to see if they are of God (1 John 4:1). The Lord revealed to me several years ago that "most of the words that have been spoken to me in my life were words of Satan." The enemy is a strategist and he will deceive those closest to us to become our enemies. For example, Satan tempted Judas to betray Christ for thirty pieces of silver. Some may ask, "do these people lose their salvation?" The Word teaches that Jesus knew from the beginning that Judas was a devil and that he did not believe (John 6:64,70). Judas was chosen by Jesus and he received the same apostolic ministry as the other disciples, but he was never a true believer. He deceived the other apostles, but Jesus knew his heart. John calls them antichrists and teaches, "They went out from us; for if they had been of us, they would have continued with us. But they went out, that it might become plain that they are not of us" (1 John 2:19). The Bible explains that there are many "tares" growing among the wheat. These weeds look like wheat until they mature and fail to bear fruit. Jesus taught that we will know them by their fruits. (Matthew 13:24-30; 36-43). I have learned that there are many "make believers" who appear to be Christians, but they will eventually turn away from God because they never truly believed.

The Bible warns us that we can fall away from any position in the Lord. God's Word records many accounts of those who began serving God and then later fell into disobedience. Many of Paul's friends walked away from God and abandoned him at the end of his life (2 Timothy 1:15). King Saul was anointed by the Holy Spirit, but he became jealous and angry, which caused him to become possessed by an evil spirit. He obeyed Satan's will to attempt to kill David, and at the end of his life he consulted a witch and then committed suicide (1 Samuel 18:5-12; 15, 28-29). Lucifer was an archangel who was called to worship and glorify God, but he became proud, which caused him to take his eyes off of the Lord and onto himself. He was created by God to be the bearer of light, but he became the deceiver of the world (see Isaiah 14 and Ezekiel 28). Solomon was the wisest man in the world and he built the temple to worship God, but he became a fool and worshiped evil idols to please his pagan wives. Samson was anointed by the Spirit to be the strongest man in the world, but Delilah turned him away from the Lord and his life ended in defeat and suicide. It has been discouraging to see how easily the enemy has deceived those whom I loved to turn against me. My wife was a prophet like Balaam who saw true visions of Jesus, but fell away from God and perished (Numbers 22-24). The enemy has tempted most of my closest friends to betray, rob, and abandon me in my time of need. One friend who was "helping" when my hip was broken in twelve places stole my pickup, equipment, bank card, and emergency money. My best friend who assisted me in the jail ministry for ten years turned away from God, stole from me, and blamed me for the loss of his house. My two best friends from my Church in Idaho betrayed me and supported the pastor as he kicked me out of the Church.

The weight of my sorrows and suffering are often too heavy for me to carry and I have learned to pray and give them to Jesus. Years ago, the Lord gave me a vision of myself carrying a huge burden that seemed like it would crush me. Jesus revealed that He had given me the grace to carry this great weight for the Church. I have learned to give Christ all of these burdens and enter into his rest (Matthew 11:28-30). I often spend several hours every day praying for healing and strength to endure the suffering and pain. Jesus will always heal our hearts from bitterness and anger when we choose to forgive and let go of the past. I describe the persecution of family, friends, Churches, ministries, and fellow Christians in my book *Warrior for Christ: Overcoming Cancer by Faith.*

The **LORD** is my rock, and my fortress, and my deliverer... Psalms 18.2

13

Walking with the Supernatural God

"Enoch walked with God; and he was not, for God took him."

Genesis 5:24

"Thus the LORD used to speak to Moses face to face, as a man
speaks to his friend."

Exodus 33:11

"If we live by the Spirit, let us also walk by the Spirit."

Galatians 5:25

Every day is a miracle when we walk with the supernatural Creator of the universe. Religion is following dead traditions and rituals of men, but a relationship with Christ is the most exciting adventure that we can ever experience. We can boldly go into the presence of God by the blood of Christ, through the new and living way that He opened for us by His death on the Cross (Hebrews 10:19-20). The Lord will draw near to us when we draw near to Him. I believe that every word of the Bible is still true today. The words of Jesus are Spirit and life, and His Word is written on my mind and my heart (Hebrews 8:10). Jesus is alive and I walk in His resurrection power every day. The Lord baptized me in His precious

Holy Spirit and He has filled me with His anointing. The Father has shown me many glorious prophecies, visions, and dreams according to His promise, "And in the last days it shall be, God declares, that I will pour out my Spirit upon all flesh, and your sons and your daughters shall prophesy, and your young men shall see visions, and your old men shall dream dreams" (Acts 2:17). The Lord has blessed me with two visions of Jesus on the white throne, one of Him after His resurrection, and another vision of Him in a white robe. The Lord has graciously given me visions of the coming of Christ and the glorious outpouring of the Spirit, called the Latter Rain, that will prepare the Church for His return. The Lord revealed to me that I am called to preach to many nations, and I have seen two visions of me speaking to a large stadium filled with people. The Lord also showed me a vision of the earth and indicated that He will send me to carry His Gospel to the world. The power of the Spirit will be so strong that I will enter a hospital and many will walk out healed. Jesus continues to anoint his Church with the baptism of the Holy Spirit to empower us to fulfill the great commission. The gifts of healing, miracles, and tongues did not end with the early Church. Those who truly believe will have a passion to know the Lord and a hunger for His Word. The presence of God makes my life glorious and without Him I am nothing. The Father has invited each of us to be His friend and walk with Him like Enoch and Moses. I prayed for many years to know Him, and the Lord has been gracious to speak to me face-to-face as a friend (Exodus 33:11). Thank you, Jesus! The Lord still calls His chosen ones as He called Moses at the burning bush. Forty-four years ago, I was called by God and He told me to take off my shoes because it was holy ground. The Lord made the hand of Moses leprous and then restored it. Similarly, the Father crippled my hands and then healed them several minutes later. Angels continue to appear to us today as they did in Biblical times. Jacob saw angels on a ladder stretching up to heaven. When the Lord called me, I was surrounded by hundreds of angels in balconies reaching up to heaven. The Lord has been protecting us with angels our entire lives. An angel appeared to me in human form when I was in college. He sat down next to me in a library with an angelic smile and encouraged me when I was feeling alone (Hebrews 13:2). Jesus continues to heal and raise the dead. As I explained in chapter six, the Lord raised me from a terminal illness and He restored me mentally, physically, and emotionally. Those who live godly lives will be persecuted today as they were in Biblical times, and I have often been rejected by Churches, ministries, and fellow Christians. The lukewarm Church is not persecuted because they are not true followers of Christ. The Father continues to open the spiritual door into heaven to permit His people to view the spiritual world beyond the veil (Revelation 4). During my seven-year illness, the Lord allowed me to see into the heavenly realm and I viewed the great spiritual battles between the angels of God and the fallen angels of the devil that affect the events that occur on this earth. Jesus continues to call us today to leave everything behind to follow Him (Matthew 4:18-22). Twenty-five years ago, Jesus asked me to leave my life in Idaho and move to Phoenix to minister to the homeless and those in nursing homes and jails. Jesus performs the same miracles today as He did in His earthly ministry. He promises that those who believe will do the works that He did (John 14:12). I have witnessed the Lord raise a man who died in hospice, and He added fifteen years to a man's life who was dying of aids in the ICU (2

Kings 20:1-5). I prayed for many years that the glory of Christ would return to the Church as in the book of Acts. Recently, the Holy Spirit has anointed me to bring many to Christ, heal the sick, and cast out many demons in online crusades in Pakistan. Recently, the Lord used me to cast out an army of demons from a man in Pakistan and deliver a woman that had been possessed for fifteen years. Many have been healed of COVID, heart and kidney issues, paralysis, diabetes, and other illnesses and injuries. God is good! Jesus still heals those who are crippled, and He calls me to rise up and walk every day with eleven fractured vertebrae. By the same power that the Lord used to feed the five thousand (John 6: 5-14), I witnessed Jesus multiply thirty-five communion cups to supply seventy inmates, and there were two leftover.. God's Word is just as powerful today as it was in Biblical times. Heaven and earth will pass away, but His Word will never pass away (Matthew 24:35). Every promise in His Word is still true today for those who believe. Jesus is the same yesterday, today, and forever (Hebrews 13:8).

Our flesh has a natural fear of the supernatural or anything that can not be religiously or intellectually explained. God has not given us a spirit of fear but of power, love, and a sound mind (2 Timothy 1:7). When the disciples saw Jesus walking on the water in the storm, they were terrified because they were afraid of the supernatural (Matthew 14:23-33). Jesus is calling us to step out of the religious boat of fear and embrace the gifts and miracles of God. Religion is dead, but Jesus is alive. I seek to know the supernatural God in all of His glory because in His presence, there is fullness of joy. If the religious god that you serve does not do miracles, then trade him in for the risen Christ. When the Creator of the universe comes into our lives, there will be an immediate and powerful change. A true born-again experience is an amazing miracle of God. At Pentecost, three thousand men and women were born again and filled with the Holy Spirit. Immediately, the Lord gave them a hunger for His Word, a passion to seek God, prayer, and fellowship with other believers (Acts 2:34-47). The early Church was led by the Spirit, experienced many encounters with angels, and was anointed with great power to heal, cast out demons, and raise the dead. Lukewarm Christianity is a dead counterfeit of a true relationship with the amazing eternal heavenly Father. Those who are "saved" in lukewarm Christianity become "stillborn babies" without the life of the Spirit. Lukewarm and worldly Christians will hear Jesus say at the end, "Depart from me, I never knew you" (Luke 13:23-27). True Christianity is not a dead religion, but an amazing relationship with the Supernatural Creator of all things. Every day is a miracle as we walk by the Spirit and experience the joy of God's presence. Thank you, Jesus!

14

Eyes of Faith

"Because we look not to the things that are seen but to
the things that are unseen, for the things that are seen are
transient, but the things that are unseen are eternal."

2 Corinthians 4:18

"By faith we understand that the world was created by the
word of God, so that what is seen was made out of things
which do not appear."

Hebrews 11:3

By faith, we understand that the invisible God is the Creator and Ruler over the physical world. The spiritual is eternal while the physical world is passing away (2 Corinthians 4:18). We start our lives without faith, believing that the physical world is real and what is invisible is an unknown mystery. When we are born again, we take a step of faith and begin to pray to an invisible God. Gradually, our faith grows and we develop a relationship with the unseen God who loves us. The Lord gives us eyes of faith to see into the spiritual realm that controls the events in this world. The book of Job teaches us that the spiritual world controls the events in our lives. Job lost his family, possessions, and servants in one day. A person without faith will often see these hardships as occurring by chance. A news reporter might report that one day a strong wind happened to blow against the house and killed all of Job's children. Randomly, thieves killed his servants and stole his possessions. On the same day, fire came down and destroyed the rest of his sheep. Job was just having a really bad day. A short time later, Job was randomly struck with a very painful skin disease and his wife turned against him and advised him to curse God and die. Many watch the news channels that report crime, natural disasters, and tragedies, but those who walk with God can see the spiritual origins of these disasters. The book of Job reveals that the Lord allowed the enemy to test Job's faith by triggering these tragedies. By faith, we realize that we are in a spiritual battle with an unseen enemy who is often behind the sickness, natural disasters, and suffering that we are experiencing on this earth. True faith looks beyond the powers of darkness to see that the Lord is in control of every event in our lives. The enemy is a pawn in the hand of the Father to refine us and burn away the flesh so that we may become more like Christ. The enemy intends to destroy us, but God is working in all things for good. The devil's plan was to tempt Job to become angry and curse God, but Job held fast to his integrity and worshiped God amid this tragedy. When Job passed the first test, Satan asked permission from God to afflict Job with a painful physical illness. In my experience, pain and sickness are the most difficult tests of my faith. The Lord allowed the devil to afflict Job, but the Father would not let him take his life. In the last chapter of the book, Job reveals what the Lord had taught him through his test of faith: "I had heard of thee by the hearing of the ear, but now my eye sees thee; therefore I despise myself, and repent in dust and ashes" (Job

42:5-6). Job had been religious, but now he was blessed with a true and intimate relationship with the Lord.

I have endured two "Job experiences." In the first one, the Father called me to walk by faith through intense suffering caused by a seven-year terminal illness. According to His promise, the Father healed me and completely restored my life. By the grace of God, my faith remained strong through this intense spiritual warfare. The Lord opened my eyes to the spiritual world that is usually hidden from our natural eyes. My body was near death, but my spirit was alive as I viewed the spiritual battle between the Lord and His angels and the devil and his demons. The baptism of fire burned away my sinful nature but did not harm who I was in Christ. During this intense spiritual warfare, the Lord gave me a spiritual sword that I used to battle these demons. In the morning, my hand would sometimes be temporarily paralyzed from gripping this sword for hours during the night. The demons were tormenting me with pain with what felt like "invisible knives." The Lord revealed to me that in the lake of fire, people will experience pain in a similar way that I did during this illness. The Father reminded me that there are no physical bodies in this next life because we leave them on this earth when we die. Jesus gave me the grace to walk with Him through this demonic war, and He carried me through the most difficult times. The Lord protected me and He revealed to me that without His grace, even Paul would have disintegrated in this battle. I endured this suffering by faith in God and in His promise to heal me. After living in this spiritual realm for seven years, the physical world appeared to be like a fake movie set used by the devil to deceive people. When Jesus healed me, I asked Him to take away some of this ability to see into the spiritual realm so that I could work and interact with the world again. Unfortunately, my wife lost her faith in the battle and decided that the devil would win. Like Job's wife, she turned away from God and fell into the deception of the enemy. I am currently going through my second "Job experience" with stage four cancer, which has caused eleven compression fractures to my spine. If I look at this cancer through my natural eyes, I will believe that it was caused by the poisonous weed killer that I utilized during my years working as a landscaper. When I walk by faith, I see that this illness is according to the plan of God, and I believe that I am called to glorify God through this cancer journey. I have been under intense spiritual attack for the past thirty months as I have endured pain and suffering. Jesus lifts me up every day and I walk in the resurrection power of Christ. The Lord has given me a vision of healing while I was walking with my walker nearly two years ago. I saw a scripture come out of heaven and into me: "He sent forth his word and healed them" (Psalm 107:20). I walk by faith every day as I wait for the Lord's promised healing.

The Lord has revealed to me that the COVID pandemic is the result of spiritual warfare. On March 8th, 2020, the enemy attempted to attack me with the COVID virus and I began to feel sick with the symptoms of the illness. I could not sleep and I prayed for most of the night. The attack intensified until I could see the demons in my room at about 3 a.m. One hour later, the Holy Spirit told me to plead for the blood of Jesus, and immediately I saw a wall of blood between me and the demons. The wall was made of large drops of the blood of Christ, and I could look through the openings to see the demons behind the wall. Thankfully, the Lord has protected me from this virus. That night, the Lord revealed to me that this last day plague was a call to repentance and He gave me the Scripture, "Come, O sons, listen to me, I will teach you the fear of the LORD" (Psalm 34:11). Recently, I prayed through the internet for six men in Pakistan who were suffering from COVID. By the grace of God, they were all saved and healed. Jesus has given us His authority to lead people to Christ and also to heal and deliver them from demons. The Word teaches that we are not battling against flesh and blood, but against demonic principalities of darkness (Ephesians 6:10-18). Unfortunately, many Christians remain ignorant of the spiritual wars that are happening all around them. Jesus told us to be wise as serpents and innocent as doves (Matthew 10:16). For instance, married couples sometimes fight and argue with each other, not realizing that their real enemy is the devil. God is calling us to rise above the darkness and spiritual blindness of this world so that we can walk by faith in the victory of Christ with the Supernatural God who rules over this earth.

Make me to know Thy ways, O LORD; teach me Thy Paths. Psalm 25.4

15

Comebacks

"Have this mind among yourselves, which is yours in Christ Jesus, who, though he was in the form of God, did not count equality with God a thing to be grasped, but emptied himself, taking the form of a servant, being born in the likeness of men. And being found in human form he humbled himself and became obedient unto death, even death on a cross. Therefore God has highly exalted him and bestowed on him the name which is above every name."

Philippians 2:5-8

"Behold, the former things have come to pass, and new things I now declare; before they spring forth I tell you of them."

Isaiah 42:9

"But he laid his right hand upon me, saying, 'Fear not, I am the first and the last, and the living one; I died, and behold I am alive for evermore, and I have the keys of Death and Hades.'"

Revelation 1:17-18

Most of us are inspired by comebacks. We cheer for the "underdog" in sporting events, and we are amazed when a team comes from behind and wins at the very end of the game. Many people are inspired by stories of bravery and courage when a person overcomes severe challenges and adversity. We admire those who refuse to give up when facing a terminal illness or a severe handicap. Biblically, we make a "comeback" by overcoming adversity through faith in Jesus. The greater the challenge, the more faith that's required to rise above it. The Bible is filled with stories of great men and women who pleased God with their faith. The Lord often uses trials to test our faith to reveal whether it is genuine (1 Peter 1:6-7). The resurrection of Christ is the ultimate example of a "comeback." Jesus spent His life on this earth, loving, healing, teaching the truth, and delivering many from demonic possession. Sadly, Jesus was rejected by the world that He created, betrayed by His own people, and crucified on the Cross. The enemy deceived the Jewish leaders to falsely accuse, mock, and murder the Son of God. The story of the Cross was the ultimate battle between good and evil, love and hate. The power of sin and death couldn't hold Him, and on the third day, He made the most amazing "comeback" in history by rising from the dead. The miraculous power of Christ's resurrection continued to work in the early Church as they overcame strong resistance from the enemy. Paul spread the Gospel to many nations, despite experiencing beatings and imprisonments. In one city, Paul was stoned and left for dead, but Jesus raised him and he continued preaching the Gospel (Acts 14:19).

The Bible is a story of ordinary men and women who were chosen by God to do extraordinary things. The Lord picked a teenage shepherd boy named David to be His king, and He chose Moses, the most humble man in the world, to lead two and a half million Israelites to the Promised Land. The Lord used a timid man named Gideon to bring victory to Israel. Jeremiah was chosen to be a mighty prophet despite his objections that he was too young and unable to speak. The Lord chose a teenage virgin named Mary to be the mother of Jesus and a barren woman named Elizabeth to be the mother of John the Baptist. Jesus called a handful of poor and uneducated disciples to change the world. They were filled with the Holy Spirit and spread the gospel to many nations. The Lord called Saul, a persecutor of the Church, to carry His Gospel to the Gentiles. God's Word teaches, "For consider your call, brethren, not many of you were wise according to worldly standard, not many were powerful, not many were of noble birth; but God chose what is foolish in the world to shame the wise, God chose what is weak in the world to shame the strong, God chose what is low and despised, even things that are not, to bring to nothing things that are, so that no human being might boast in the presence of God" (1 Corinthians 1:26-29). Faith is believing in God and trusting that He will deliver us from the most difficult circumstances. The enemy has sought to destroy my life, but the Lord has delivered me from all evil. I have learned that faith never gives up, even while experiencing difficult challenges.

I have been knocked down many times in my life, but by the grace of God, Jesus has always raised me up. The Father healed me from a seven-year illness that destroyed my body, erased my memory, and caused severe mental illness. At the appointed time, the resurrection power of Christ entered into me and healed my body, mind, and heart. The Lord restarted my life from the beginning and I learned how to walk, talk, read and write again. Jesus restored my memory, healed my heart, and gave me back my ability to ski, climb mountains, hike, and bike ride. I had lived seven years in extreme poverty, but the Lord restored my landscaping business and blessed me financially. The Lord miraculously healed me when my hip was broken in twelve places. Recently, the Father chose to test my faith again with terminal stage four cancer that caused eleven compression fractures of my vertebrae. The illness took away my job, ministry, and even my ability to walk. The illness completely immobilized me, and I spent five months sitting in a chair with extreme pain from the fractures. When I was diagnosed with stage four cancer, people began planning my funeral, and I heard a voice telling me that I had served God for twenty-five years and it was time to go home. I realized that this voice was the lying deception of the devil telling me to give up. I decided to live by this cancer motto: "Give the cancer to God, live one day at a time, and try to help as many people as I can every day." I cried out to Jesus for mercy, and the Lord heard my prayer and He began to heal me. Cancer is strong, but Jesus is stronger! Currently, the Lord has called me to make another "comeback" as I began to preach the gospel on the internet in 2020. The Lord anointed me to preach the Gospel twenty-five years ago, but the cancer severely impaired my memory and my ability to speak. For the first year, few listened and some even mocked me. I deleted the first one hundred videos, but I continued to preach by faith. By faith, I persisted, and the Lord has graciously opened doors for me to preach to thousands at crusades in Pakistan. God's strength is made perfect in weakness, and the Lord has anointed me to preach the Gospel, heal the sick, and cast out demons. Thank you, Jesus!

16

Ministry: Bless all the Nations

"Arise, shine; for your light has come, and the glory of the
LORD has risen upon you. For behold, darkness shall cover
the earth, and thick darkness the peoples; but the LORD will
arise upon you, and his glory will be seen upon you. And the
nations shall come to your light, and kings to the brightness
of your rising."

Isaiah 60:1-3

"And this gospel of the kingdom will be preached throughout
the whole world, as a testimony to all nations; and then the
end will come."

Matthew 24:14

Forty-four years ago, the Lord spoke to me, "Thou art my chosen one" and "Thou shall bless all the nations." I was surrounded by angels and the Father told me to take off my shoes because I was standing on holy ground. I was only twenty-four years old, and I was amazed that God would choose me to bless all the nations. For the past forty-four years, I have lived by faith, believing that the Lord would fulfill this promise. My faith has been tested with a seven-year terminal illness and stage four cancer which caused

Our fourteenth crusade in Pakistan.

eleven compression fractures to my back. I was crippled from the disease and it seemed improbable that this vision would be fulfilled, but with God all things are possible. The Lord was testing my faith, but like Abraham, I believed that God would do the impossible: "In hope he believed against hope, that he should become the father of many nations; as he had been told, 'So shall your descendants be.' He did not weaken in faith when he considered his own body, which was as good as dead because he was about a hundred years old, or when he considered the barrenness of Sarah's womb. No distrust made him waver concerning the promise of God, but he grew strong in his faith as he gave glory to God, fully convinced that God was able to do what he had promised" (Romans 4:18-20). For the first year of ministry in Pakistan, there were small audiences, frequent cancellations, and many services were cut short by poor internet connections. I persevered and the Lord connected me to Pastor Nasir from Pakistan who has been a great blessing to me. His family has the same vision of preaching God's Word to many nations. With his assistance, the Lord has graciously opened up a door for me to preach online at thirteen large crusades to thousands of people. Pastor Nasir and his crew find the location, set up the crusades, schedules bus transportation, and arrange for the food distribution to the poor. His wife translates my message into the native language. His four sisters and the rest of the family pray every day for me and the ministry. The whole family have been an amazing blessing to me, and I pray and fellowship with this pastor and his family for several hours a day. Thank you, Lord! The following paragraph shows Pastor Nasir and his wife distributing sweaters to the orphans and poor children at our Christmas Crusade.

I was near death, but the Lord has raised me and anointed me to share the Gospel with many nations. For the last month, the Lord has graciously allowed me to stand up and preach with a broken back. After waiting by faith for forty-four years, the Lord has begun to fulfill His vision for me to bless the nations. God is good! Jesus has given me His authority to preach the Word, heal the sick, and cast out demons. Jesus proclaimed, "'All authority in heaven and on earth has been given to me. Go therefore and make disciples of all nations, baptizing them in the name of the Father and of the Son and of the Holy Spirit, teaching them to observe all that I have commanded you; and lo, I am with you always, to the close of the age'" (Matthew

28:18-20). The Lord has poured out His Spirit with the power to be His witnesses and fulfill the Great Commission (Acts 1:9). It appeared that my time on earth was ending, but my new life is just beginning because with God, all things are possible! By the grace of God, the Lord has opened doors to preach online at many crusades in Pakistan where hundreds were saved, and many were healed and delivered from demons. Men and women are baptized with the Holy Spirit and speak in tongues. The Lord is pouring out His Spirit as in the days of the early Church. Hallelujah! God's ways are amazing— He has anointed me with the gift of healing while I am suffering from stage four cancer and a crippled back. God is great! Thank you, Jesus! God's grace is sufficient and His power is made perfect in weakness. Cancer is my thorn in the flesh which keeps me weak so that God's power can work through me. Paul wrote, "And to keep me from being too elated by the abundance of revelations, a thorn was given me in the flesh, a messenger of Satan, to harass me, to keep me from being too elated. Three times I besought the Lord about this, that it should leave me; but he said to me, 'My grace is sufficient for you, for my power is made perfect in weakness.' I will all the more gladly boast of my weaknesses, that the power of Christ may rest upon me. For the sake of Christ, then, I am content with weaknesses, insults, hardships, persecutions, and calamities; for when I am weak, then I am strong" (2 Corinthians 12:7-11). The Father has called me to heal many people with pain, injuries, cancer, COVID, kidney and heart issues, and diabetes. In a recent crusade, the Lord healed a baby who was paralyzed and unable to hear or speak. Praise God! Last week, Jesus healed a boy who was in the ICU with spinal meningitis. He was unresponsive and was not expected to live. As we prayed, he came alive, opened his eyes, and started moving. He is now completely healed. Thank you, Jesus. Many come to our crusades oppressed, possessed, and afflicted with many diseases, and Jesus does a miracle in their lives.

We are in a spiritual battle with the enemy for the souls of thousands of people lost in the darkness of the world. The Holy Spirit is

drawing thousands to our crusades and many are saved, healed, delivered from demons, and filled with the Spirit. I have faced much oppression and spiritual warfare in my life, and the Spirit has given me the authority in Christ to deliver those who are possessed by demons. One demon-possessed man traveled eight hours to be set free from an army of demons. He had gone to several Churches for help, but they could not deliver him. I commanded that the demons leave in the name of Jesus, and the man fell on the ground and the demons were cast out. The Lord recently used me to deliver a woman who was possessed by a demon for fifteen years. In the name of Jesus, she was set free. At our eleventh crusade, a man who had been possessed by an army of demons for twenty years was delivered. Many people testify that they had gone to other crusades and Churches for deliverance but they had not been set free. They express their joy and gratitude that they were finally free from these evil spirits. Amen! Thank you, Jesus! We recently held a Christmas Crusade where we distributed sweaters to about two hundred orphans and poor children, and about fifty widows received prayer and a large bag of food. I asked Biblical questions, and those who answered correctly received a cash prize. Thank you, Jesus, for this beautiful crusade!

I have prayed for many years for God's glory to return to the Church as in the days of the early Church. God's Word teaches that Jesus has given His authority to the Church so that, by faith, we can do the works that Jesus did on this earth (John 14:12). Jesus has given me His authority to preach the gospel to many nations, heal the sick, and cast out demons. The Lord has prepared me for this ministry for over forty years—all glory goes to Him. I have no power to bring people to Christ, heal or deliver—it is all Jesus. The Father has called me to proclaim the Gospel to many nations to fulfill His plan to gather the Church before Christ's return. I believe that this ministry to Pakistan is the beginning of a worldwide ministry for God's glory. Jesus will heal me and send me to share His love with the world. Praise God! Thank you Jesus for your grace and mercy. The Lord is amazing, and with Him all things are possible!

Update: God Bless All Nations Ministry is a miracle from God. Seven years ago, I was completely paralyzed after cancer collapsed eleven vertebrae, but God told me to stand up and walk because He was sending me to preach the Gospel and bless many nations. With God, all things are possible! By the grace of God, as of November 2024, this ministry has conducted about 120 Crusades in Pakistan with thousands saved, healed, and delivered from demons. God is pouring out His latter rain anointing for the last day harvest before Jesus returns. Thousands come to these crusades from various religious backgrounds in a land of great spiritual darkness and oppression. Many of them come to Christ when they hear the Gospel and see the light of His glory and power to do mighty miracles. Many teenage girls who are possessed by demons through black magic are delivered and completely restored. Hundreds of people come to these crusades crying out to be delivered from demons and they are all healed by Jesus. Crippled men and women are touched by Jesus and run up and down the aisles. A boy who had never spoken began repeating, "Hallelujah, Hallelujah." The blind come to Jesus and receive perfect eyesight. Jesus has healed many from cancer, diabetes, heart disease, liver and kidney disease, and countless other illnesses. God has answered the prayers of hundreds to receive baby blessings. I prayed for over forty years to see God's glory come back into the

Church as in the days of the gospels and the early Church. Thank you, Jesus! By the grace of God, we have started a Church for an entire village of 150 Hindus who have converted from idols to Christ. They lived in a desert without electricity or water and were forced to travel several hours each day to obtain water. God has allowed us to provide three wells for the village and many audio Bibles to help them learn the Word of God. They worship God regularly using a drum that we provided for them on our last visit. Thank you, Jesus, for your faith-fulness to do this mighty work. All glory goes to God!

The cake at the Christmas Crusade for widows and orphans.

Our third crusade for Christ in Pakistan many were where saved, healed and delivered.

Our eighth crusade in Pakistan—the glory of God fell upon us with great miracles!

17

Called to Glory

"For this slight momentary affliction is preparing for us an
eternal weight of glory beyond all comparison."

2 Corinthians 4:17

"I consider that the sufferings of this present time are not
worth comparing with the glory that is to be revealed to us."

Romans 8:18

These are the days of the great harvest of souls before Christ returns. The door to heaven is still open, and Jesus has called us to carry the good news of the Gospel to all nations and invite them to spend eternity in God's glorious presence. The Lord has commanded us to obey this great commission and to preach His Gospel to many nations. The Father has already opened the door for me to preach to thousands of men and women in Pakistan, and hundreds of people have already prayed to accept Christ as their Savior—to God be the glory! God is love and His desire is for all to be saved. The Father is pouring out His Spirit to anoint His servants to bring in the harvest of souls—for the time is short and Jesus is coming soon. "And this gospel of the kingdom will be preached throughout the whole world, as a testimony to all nations; and then the end will come" (Matthew 24:14). For several decades, the Lord has given me visions of a great outpouring of the Holy Spirit called the Latter Rain. In Israel, there was an early rain when they planted their crops and the latter rain at the time of the harvest. The early rain was the first outpouring of the Spirit at Pentecost, at the beginning of the age of grace. The Latter Rain will come at the end of the age to empower, purify, and gather the Church to prepare them for the return of Christ. This outpouring of the Spirit will be more glorious than Pentecost because Jesus is appearing as the exalted and glorified King of all the earth. Twenty-five years ago, the Lord gave me a vision that this anointing will be so powerful that I will enter into a hospital and many people will walk out healed. The Father showed me that I was like a flower that lies dormant in the desert and then comes alive when the rain comes. The Spirit of the Lord is beginning to anoint me with the power of the Latter Rain. Amen!

The Father is pouring out His Spirit to prepare the Bride of Christ for the coming of the Bridegroom. In the mid-seventies, the Lord gave me a vision of a sanctified Church rising out of the ashes of the rubble of the dead, apostate, and lukewarm church. The Bridegroom is calling His Bride to arise by the power of the Spirit and come to Him: "Arise, shine; for Your light has come, and the glory of the Lord has risen upon you. For behold, darkness shall cover the earth, and thick darkness the peoples; but the Lord will arise upon you, and His glory will be seen upon you. And nations shall come to your light, and kings to the brightness of Your rising" (Isaiah 60:1-3). Behold, the Bridegroom comes full of passion and glory! Awaken from your sleep, O my people, for He comes for His Bride. Break the chains of darkness and open your eyes to see Your King in His glory. He will clothe you will fine linen (the righteous deeds of His people) and embrace you with His love. You will no longer be afraid, for the Bridegroom will keep you safe in His arms. When Jesus removes evil from His kingdom, then the Bride will shine bright with His glory (Matthew 13:41-43). The Word proclaims, "they will see the Son of man coming on the clouds of heaven with power and great glory; and He will send out His angels with a loud trumpet call, and they will gather His elect from the four winds, from one end of heaven to the other" (Matthew 24:30-31). The word "angel" can be translated "messenger," and the Lord is sending out his servants, anointed by the Spirit, to gather His Church and prepare them for His return. The miracle has already begun, and I have seen hundreds come to Christ in Pakistan. Those whose names are written in the book of life before the foundation of the world will believe in Jesus, awaken from their sleep, and rise up unto eternal life (Revelation 13:8). Amen! The light of the Gospel will open their eyes and deliver them from the darkness of this present age. The power of the Holy Spirit will sanctify the Bride and cleanse her "by the washing of water with the word, that he might present the church to himself in splendor, without spot or wrinkle or any such thing, that she might be holy and without blemish" (Ephesians 5:26-27). Jesus is calling His Church out of the kingdom of this world (Egypt) into a new heavenly land. Jesus is shouting, "Let my people go," and the devil (Pharaoh) is resisting the plan of God. The enemy seeks to keep God's people in slavery to sin and bondage under the oppression of this present darkness. They cry out for a deliverer. Behold, He comes to deliver His people from slavery and take them to His heavenly kingdom. Jesus will set His people free by the power of His blood and by the great outpouring of His Holy Spirit to gather His Church. The Savior comes and He will break their chains of deception and bondage to sin. The Lord will place His Church in the safety of His Presence forever.

My prayer for the Church is: "O Lord, pour out Your Spirit upon Your people and fill our hearts with a passion to know You. Let Your people fall in love with Jesus and let His presence fill their souls. Call Your people out of this world and draw them to You forever. Gather your Church that is lost in darkness and deliver them from the power of the enemy and the bondage of sin. Let them lay down their idols and bow down to the one true living God who loves His people with an everlasting love. By Your grace, cause Your Church to rise up with the power of the Spirit and become an exceedingly great army. Send forth Your messengers to gather Your Bride from the four corners of heaven and let them come together as one people united in Your love. May Your Spirit draw them out of this world to sit with You in heavenly places. Purify their hearts that the light of Jesus may shine forth out of His Bride. Remove from us the love for this world and replace it with a pure and holy devotion to You. Pour out a baptism of fire to burn away our flesh by the power of the Holy Spirit. Make us a Bride full of holiness and without blemish awaiting the coming of the Bridegroom. Let us be clothed with the righteousness of Christ. Sanctify and cleanse us with the washing of Your holy Word and prepare us as Your Bride adorned for her husband."

When I first moved to Phoenix, the Lord gave me a vision of the amazing resurrection power of Christ's second coming. I was standing outside a local Church and the Lord raised me up and filled me with the all-knowing, all-powerful eternal Spirit of God. I was lifted up in the Spirit about fifty feet off the ground and I could see myself still standing on the ground. The power of God in me was far greater than the bondage of sin, death, sickness, and the devil. I have kept this vision in my heart through many years of suffering. This age of suffering will soon come to an end, and we will enter into the new age of eternal glory. Those who sow in tears will reap with shouts of joy (Psalms 126:5). The sorrow of this life will fade away in the presence of our heavenly Father. "I consider that the sufferings of this present time are not worth comparing with the glory that is to be revealed to us" (Romans 8:18). Jesus will give us new resurrection bodies that can never die, experience pain, or grow old. The Father will make us righteous in Christ and remove all the effects of sin in our hearts and minds.

The seventh trumpet will soon sound, and the great King will reign on earth with all His Saints who have longed for His appearing (Revelation 11:15). "And the kingdom and the dominion and the greatness of the kingdoms under the whole heaven shall be given to the people of the saints of the Most High; their kingdom shall be an everlasting kingdom, and all dominions shall serve and obey them" (Daniel 7:27). I look forward to exploring God's new creation with my father, who has been with the Lord for forty-two years. We will see God's face and shine with His eternal glory, and we will share this reward with all the amazing believers who have walked with God on this earth. The living water of the Holy Spirit will flow into us with joy forevermore. I will be able to walk and run without pain. I will climb those beautiful mountains and talk with the Father always. The Father has promised to meet me on a hill in heaven to talk with me and answer all of my questions. The Lord will then reveal to us His glorious plan for the rest of eternity.

"The Lord will rescue me from every evil and save me for his heavenly kingdom. To him be the glory for ever and ever. Amen" (2 Timothy 4:18). When Christ returns, I will stand in my allotted place which has been prepared by the Father (Daniel 12:13). Many years ago, the Lord revealed to me my position in His kingdom, but He has asked me not to share this while I am on this earth. The Lord is coming with glory and all things will be revealed. Hallelujah! When Jesus appears, we will shout in victory, "'O death, where is thy victory: O death where is thy sting?' The sting of death is sin and the power of sin is the law. But thanks be to God, who gives us the victory through our Lord Jesus Christ" (1 Corinthians 15:55-57). I will worship Him with all believers, "Worthy is the Lamb who was slain, to receive power and wealth and wisdom and might and honor and glory and blessing!" (Revelation 5:12). Hallelujah! Come, Lord Jesus, come!

The Lord's promise to me four years ago:
"You will rise, Peter; you will rise above them all."

One year ago He spoke to me:
"You will be the one who rises, Peter."

God, the LORD, is my strength; He makes my feet like hind's feet, He makes me tread upon my high places.
Habakkuk 3.19

Also by Peter Schuler

In Pursuit of God: A Love Story

Forty-one years ago, the Lord put a passion in the heart of Peter Schuler to seek God with all his heart, soul, and strength. By Grace, the Father has revealed Himself to Peter in a glorious way through visions, revelation, and amazing times of fellowship in the Presence of the Lord. Follow Peter's journey to know God as he worships the Father with music and photography on majestic mountain tops and beside beautiful lakes and streams. It is Peter's prayer that this book will inspire others to fall in love with Christ and begin their own journey to know Him. The Father Loves us more than we can ever know. Once you experience the True Presence of God, nothing else will ever satisfy.

Also by Peter Schuler

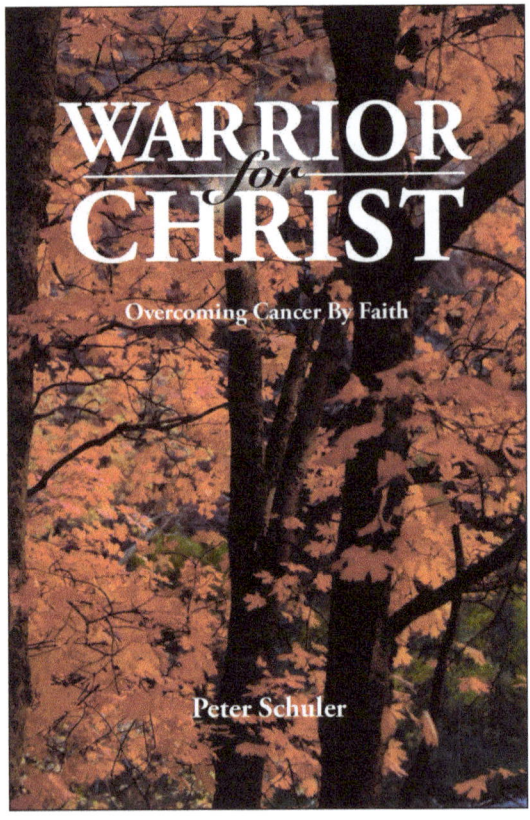

Warrior for Christ: Overcoming Cancer By Faith

Warrior for Christ: Overcoming Cancer by Faith is the inspirational story of how Peter Schuler is walking by faith in God to overcome incurable Stage 4 cancer that has caused eleven compression fractures of his vertebrae. Every day, Jesus does a miracle and lifts Peter up to walk with severe back pain. This book describes how Jesus has healed Peter of a near-terminal illness, a crippling injury, and childhood trauma. Peter shares how Jesus called him twenty-five years ago to minister to the homeless and those in jails and nursing homes.

www.ingramcontent.com/pod-product-compliance
Lightning Source LLC
Chambersburg PA
CBHW051527120626
46551CB00012B/1109